BEREAVEMENT

BEREAVEMENT

*Counseling
the Grieving
throughout
the Life Cycle*

David A. Crenshaw, Ph.D.

Foreword by William Van Ornum

Crossroad | New York

1995
The Crossroad Publishing Company
370 Lexington Avenue
New York, NY 10017

Printed in the United States of America

Library of Congress Cataloging-in-Publication Data

Crenshaw, David A.
    Bereavement : counseling the grieving throughout the
life cycle /
David A. Crenshaw ; foreword by William Van Ornum.
        p.   cm.—
    Includes bibliographical references.
    0-8245-1291-X (pbk.)
    1. Grief   2. Grief in children.   3. Bereavement—Psychological
aspects.   4. Bereavement in children.   5. Counseling.   I. Title.
II. Series.
BF575.G7C74   1990
155.9'37—dc20   89-49671
                                                                      CIP

Grateful acknowledgment is made to Brunner/Mazel, Inc., for permission to quote from *Therapeutic Metaphors for Children and the Child Within*
by Joyce C. Mills and Richard J. Crowley. Copyright 1986 by Joyce C.
Mills and Richard J. Crowley. Reprinted with permission from Brunner/
Mazel, Inc.

To my encouraging and supportive family:
my wife Mary,
my daughters: Stefanie and Gillian,
and my parents: J. V. and Genevieve Crenshaw

Contents

Foreword

David Crenshaw brings nearly two decades of clinical experience to this book on bereavement through the life cycle. As a psychologist he has worked with people of all ages who grieve the various losses of life. In his work at the Astor Home for Children he is able to take insights gathered from an extreme group of sorrowful children—those in residential placement because of multiple losses or other traumas in their lives. Understanding the grief of children helps to understand all losses throughout life.

This book will be helpful to everyone, including experienced therapists, who will benefit from Crenshaw's overview of different types of grieving during different life stages. This is a unique feature of the book, which helps to set it apart from the many other books on bereavement that are available.

Crenshaw provides myriad practical suggestions for helping us to understand the grief of others, and does so without encouraging a "cookbook" approach that might seem facile in dealing with profound losses. He provides readers with an understanding of the seven tasks of mourning, and discusses the consequences of unresolved grief and the importance of social contacts.

The chapters on helping children and teenagers deal

with grief are especially helpful. Crenshaw includes metaphors and examples from stories to help explain the grieving process to children, and these will assist the reader to be truthful and compassionate.

Throughout the book there are many case examples that illustrate bereavement and constructive interventions when dealing with people throughout the continuum of the life cycle, from childhood through adolescence and adulthood to old age. Special types of grieving are considered, such as the early death of a spouse, death by miscarriage, and death of an adult child, and these examples further provide the reader with an outlook of compassion and understanding.

Readers with an interest in the theoretical components of grieving will find reference to important work by Bowlby and the Harvard Bereavement Project.

Sometimes a support group of persons who have experienced a similar loss can be very healing, and Crenshaw provides an appendix of such groups, including The Compassionate Friends (for bereaved parents).

This is a book to be read thoroughly, and to be a reference companion to the counselor or interested adult who is faced with helping someone through the grief process. David Crenshaw's considerable skills as a clinician are evident throughout, and his insight, intelligence, and compassion will help all of us when we need to help others to cope with separation and loss.

William Van Ornum, Ph.D.
Marist College
Poughkeepsie, New York

Preface

This book is written for all who work with grieving children and adults. Social workers, teachers, therapists, members of the clergy, physicians and nurses, guidance counselors, hospice workers, funeral directors, parents, relatives, and friends—are all confronted sooner or later with the need to comfort and help a grieving child or adult.

For the past eighteen years I have worked in the residential treatment of emotionally disturbed children many of whom are grieving in their own way multiple losses, often consisting of the death or abandonment of one or both natural parents. The losses compound with subsequent placements in multiple foster homes and frequent separations from siblings and other family members culminating in their placement in residential treatment when their disturbance is deemed to be too serious to be dealt with in the community. Many of these children are chronically grieving behind the mask of various forms of behavioral acting out, often consisting of angry, defiant actions.

In my private practice as a clinical psychologist during the past twelve years, I have frequently worked with children and adults who manifested various symptoms and adjustment difficulties that proved to be related to delayed and unresolved grief. As a consequence, I have attempted to learn all that I can about helpful ways to intervene. In reviewing the professional literature, I found a few books on bereavement counseling, but most are not geared to helpers who may have received little clinical training but nevertheless are often among the frontline caregivers to whom the majority of grievers will turn in their acute pain. Most bereaved people do not turn to therapists but rather to their clergy, their funeral director, school counselor, social worker, doctor, or nurse. Only the cases of complicated bereavement typically are seen by trained therapists. This book is meant to be a practical guide for caregivers. I grew up in a small farming community in Missouri and have always valued a "down-to-earth" approach. Considerable attention is given to what you actually say to a three-year-old whose mother has just died. A concerted effort has been made to avoid professional jargon throughout.

Even less is available in the professional literature regarding developmental considerations as it pertains to bereavement. Since the death of a parent when the child is five is a very different experience from losing a parent at age forty-five, helpers need as a practical guide ready access to pertinent developmental information. This book is written from a life-cycle framework. Each phase of the life cycle poses unique challenges and exacts certain requirements for healthy growth and development. The beginning chapter examines issues and presents guidelines pertaining to grieving at all ages and is followed by three chapters examining grieving in different stages of childhood and then three chapters exploring grieving and ways of intervening in different stages of adult life.

I am indebted to many people for their encouragement and support in undertaking this work. Ray A. Craddick has been a source of inspiration and encouragement from the beginning of my career right up to the present. Walter

Bonime has for the past eight years in psychotherapy supervision offered me many rich clinical insights from his vast experience and has influenced many of the ideas developed in this book. I am grateful to John B. Mordock for encouraging me to write and for being an inspiring role model. I wish to acknowledge the helpful and enthusiastic assistance of the editor of this series, William Van Ornum, throughout this project.

Special thanks go to the children, families, staff, and administration at the Astor Home for Children and my private psychotherapy patients for providing me with the clinical experiences that made this work possible. The Astor Home for Children since 1953 has been providing hope to young people and their families through a wide variety of inpatient, outpatient, and preventative services. The current executive director is Sister Marie Burns, and the assistant executive director in charge of the residential treatment programs is Walter Joseph. More specific acknowledgment goes to those who read early drafts of the chapters and made helpful suggestions, including the following colleagues at the Astor Home for Children: Walt Chrisman, Herb Kaplan, Martha Parker, Laurie Worth, Drs. Linda Tafapolsky, Anne Campbell, Annie Scott, Jim McGuirk, Lenore Strocchia-Rivera, and Lillian Lanzafame. I especially wish to thank Chris Foreacre who read all the chapters and offered many helpful ideas. My thanks also go to Ken and Karen Giek for their willingness to read and critique the introductory chapter.

I am grateful to Theresa Brettschneider, librarian at the Astor Home for Children, for her helpful assistance as well as the Southeastern New York Library Resources Council. In addition, I wish to thank Helen Canevari and Shirley Stenberg for their secretarial assistance.

My gratitude also goes to Michael Leach, Bruce Cassiday, and Evander Lomke at Crossroad/Continuum for their extremely helpful assistance.

Finally, my appreciation goes to my wife, Mary, and daughters, Stefanie and Gillian, for their patience, understanding, support, and helpful ideas throughout this project.

Author's Note

The identities of the people written about in this book have been carefully disguised in accordance with professional standards of confidentiality and in keeping with their rights to privileged communication with the author.

1

The Need to Grieve throughout the Life Cycle

When Bobby was eight his mother consulted me after catching him setting a minor fire in the neighbor's backyard. Bobby's father had died of a cerebral hemorrhage when Bobby was only five. At the time he showed little overt grief, even though he was very close to his father and did many things with him. One of the last straws in Bobby's case was the serious illness of his grandfather, to whom he was quite attached. Another last straw was overhearing an argument in which separation was threatened between his mother and her live-in boyfriend. After a very difficult time initially accepting this new man in his mother's life, Bobby had gradually become attached to him. The two of them shared an avid interest in sports, especially baseball. These two threatened losses, combined with the earlier unresolved, painful loss of his father evoked intense feelings of anger, sadness, and anxiety that culminated in the symptomatic fire-setting behavior. In the very first session, when asked about the loss of his father and the things he missed about him, Bobby broke down and sobbed for a long time, finally giving expression to his long-avoided grief. During subsequent sessions, Bobby was able to work gradually through his feelings

19

of loss regarding his father. This made it somewhat more bearable for him to cope with the ensuing death of his grandfather and the departure of his mother's boyfriend.

Throughout life we all face one inescapable issue: separation and loss. The natural process of growth and development leads to inevitable separations and losses as we move from one stage of life to another. In addition to the separations and losses associated with growth and development, there are, of course, unavoidable losses of those we love. These losses, so very painful, often untimely and unexpected, require us to mourn in order to achieve a healthy resolution. The capacity to mourn is partly determined by developmental factors. Some clinicians believe that the capacity to mourn is not fully developed until at least adolescence if not adulthood.[1] Other writers have noted the capacity of children as young as three and even six months of age to mourn.[2] Children do mourn but in a manner, quite different from adults, that is determined by both the cognitive and emotional development of the child.[3] Thus, if we are to help the bereaved to grieve *we must understand the developmental influences at each stage of the life cycle.* This book is organized according to a life-cycle perspective from infancy to old age. Each chapter begins with a discussion of pertinent developmental considerations, followed by a review of the impact of special losses at that particular life stage and specific recommendations and strategies for helping the bereaved. Grief counseling can be done in many settings such as a professional office, the hospital or hospice, or the bereaved family's home. While grief counseling can take many forms—such as groups led by professionals, the use of trained volunteers, or self-help groups led by bereaved people—this book will emphasize counseling of individuals and families by helping professionals. Another central aim of this book is to offer practical guidelines and strategies for all frontline caregivers who are called on to help the bereaved. The work you do is essential, often rewarding, and inevitably demanding. I hope this book will ease the enormity of the task you face in counseling the bereaved.

Bonds of Attachment

John Bowlby has written extensively about the universal tendency of human beings as well as other mammals to form attachment bonds from the earliest days of life.[4] These bonds are formed initially with our parents and other nurturing and protective figures in our early lives. Later, these attachment bonds develop in relation to intimate partners and children of our own. It is these bonds of attachment that are the source of much joy, pleasure, and meaning. It is also true that the breaking of these bonds through loss or disruption can cause some of the most intense pain that we experience. In the face of loss, when these bonds of attachment are disrupted, we have a need to grieve or mourn. This need exists not only for the adult but also for the child, even the very young one. Grief and mourning will be used interchangeably in this book and are defined as the intellectual and emotional processes that gradually lessen the psychological bond to the deceased loved one, enabling the bereaved to accept the loss and move forward.

Seven Tasks of Mourning

Although there is much disagreement and controversy about the capacity to mourn at different developmental stages, there is general agreement in the field that healthy resolution of loss requires the person to grieve and mourn. Drawing from the writings of experts in the field of bereavement and from clinical experience, I will propose seven important tasks of mourning.

Task 1: Acknowledge the Reality of the Loss

A person cannot begin the grieving process until he has first accepted the reality of the loss. In the case of very painful or sudden unexpected losses the need to deny the reality can be very strong not only for the young child but for the adult as well.[5]

Task 2: Identify and Express the Emotions of Grief

The bereaved must be helped to experience the pain of grief. This crucial aspect of the grief work consists of expressing in words the intense feelings that accompany the loss of someone important to us. The healing process is very much aided when the feelings are shared with a trusted person. When the bereaved share feelings of grief, they are not just ventilating powerful painful emotions, more importantly in terms of the healing process, they are making an active declaration of trust.

Thus, the bereaved are taking a formidable risk. Grievers are confiding and unburdening their painful feelings and thereby are expressing the belief that their feelings can be accepted and understood by significant others. This declaration of trust removes barriers of isolation, cynicism, and mistrust that so easily get erected after a tragic loss heightens our sense of vulnerability.

Task 3: Commemorating the Loss

All cultures have developed rituals and customs of mourning to assist the grieving process. Planning and participating in the funeral and burial services are helpful steps in honoring the memory of the deceased loved one. In addition the griever may need help in finding an acceptable way to remember and honor the life of a loved one who had died.[6] This can be particularly helpful when there is an undue burden of guilt in relation to the death.

Task 4: Acknowledging Ambivalence

The bereaved need to recognize and acknowledge the conflicting feelings in relation to the deceased loved one. Denial of these conflicting feelings represents a considerable barrier to the resolution of grief. Yet when someone we love dies, it rarely leaves a clean wound. Almost always, there is a mixture of intense feelings. In addition to love of the deceased, there may be anger related to the perception of desertion through death. Often the death of a loved one is emotionally experienced as an abandonment by those left behind. This may be felt especially by children or adults who had a highly dependent relationship with the deceased. In addition there may be long-standing and unexpressed resentments related to disappointments in the relationship.

The acknowledgment of these feelings is a crucial step in the mourning process. But it is very difficult, especially for children, to recognize and accept such feelings in themselves, let alone share them with someone else—even a highly trusted person. This step, then, constitutes one of the greatest challenges to helping grieving children and adults alike.

Task 5: Resolution of the Ambivalence

The griever must achieve a balance between the conflicting feelings so that both positive and negative feelings are fully recognized and then put into perspective. Some bereaved persons will express the positive feelings much more easily and will have a hard time recognizing and expressing the negative feelings. For such persons, the unacceptable and denied hostile feelings will block their attempts to resolve their grief. Counselors who have found it easy to get such individuals to talk about the things they miss about the deceased will then need to ask, "What don't you miss about the deceased?"[7]

Some grieving persons may experience the opposite. If their relationship with the deceased was unfulfilling or perhaps depriving or abusive they may find it far easier to express their hostile feelings than to express any warm or loving ones. Yet in most cases, the warm tender feelings exist unnoticed. It becomes a vital task for the grief counselor to bring these feelings into awareness and to help the mourner achieve a realistic balance between them.

Task 6: Letting Go

This task consists of saying good-bye on an emotional rather than an intellectual level. This can happen only after all the previous steps have been mastered. The bereaved must withdraw their emotional investment in the deceased in order to go forward with their lives.[8]

Task 7: Moving On

This step requires the adoption of a present and future orientation as hopes, dreams, plans, and aspirations are restructured and reshaped in view of the new realities.

This step can be exceedingly difficult because it involves relinquishing the hopes, dreams, plans, and aspirations that revolved around the deceased loved person. Sometimes this move forward can be blocked by what Bonime[9] describes as *angry unwillingness,* the person's fight against the utilization of personal resources.

In the context of bereavement, this resistance to moving on may result from anger that life has dealt the bereaved a cruel blow. The feeling of having been cheated may lead to stubborn refusal to go forward with life. Moving on can also be blocked by faulty identifications. For example, grievers may insist on viewing themselves as *tragic figures.* The bereaved must commit to full participation in life again, which may be difficult if they have received enormous gratifications from the solicitations of family and friends. These two dynamic elements can thwart the grief counselor's efforts to help grievers to move ahead.

These seven tasks of mourning are impacted by developmental factors as well as other variables including the circumstances and timing of the death and the preexisting personality of the griever. The younger the child the more likely he will have difficulty undertaking these tasks and the more he will need adult modeling, guidance, and direction. When death is untimely and sudden, the first two tasks, recognition of the reality of the loss and identification and expression of feelings, are likely to be especially difficult due to shock and denial. When the relationship between the deceased and the bereaved was highly conflicted tasks 4, acknowledgment of ambivalence, and 5, resolution of the ambivalence, are likely to pose significant challenges. When the bereaved experiences undue guilt related to the loss, task 3, commemoration, becomes especially critical. When the bereaved was excessively dependent on the deceased loved one, he/she may find task

6, letting go, and task 7, moving on, to be particularly hard.

The Consequences of Unresolved Grief

If the mourning process is skipped, avoided, or inter-rupted before closure, the person is at risk for manifesting either *delayed or distorted grief reactions.* In delayed reactions, the bereaved may show little or no outward signs of mourning at the time of a significant loss, only to react with profound grief at a later time in response to a loss of seemingly less significance. In the case of distorted grief, again the bereaved may show few signs of intense grief at the time of loss but later develop psychosomatic symptoms such as migraines or dizzy spells. They may become irritable and angry in their interpersonal rela-tionships, sometimes leading to serious conflicts. It is com-mon for couples to get a divorce within a year after the death of a child. Unable to deal with their grief, they dis-place their rage onto each other. Unexpressed resentments prior to the loss loom as significant divisive issues. A major goal of grief counseling is to prevent subsequent psychopathology by helping the bereaved to mourn their loss fully. In my practice, whenever adult patients share a plan to leave their spouse, to change jobs, to relocate, or to make any other major change in their lives, I always review with them any significant losses they have experi-enced over the past three years. Very often they will then describe the death of a parent, a close friend, a sibling, or perhaps a child for whom they were unable to mourn fully. I ask them to delay plans for major changes in their lives until they have completed the grief work. Most change their minds and are glad they did not go ahead with their original plans to alter their lives radically.

The Final Straw

When we are unwilling or unable to mourn the loss of loved ones, we are at risk for distorted or delayed grief reactions. As we attempt to go forward with life, sooner or later an event occurs that brings the unresolved grief into focus, sometimes with startling intensity. These events can be thought of as "final straws."[10] The final straw may be any subsequent loss such as another death, divorce, abortion, or life transition. This life transition may include pregnancy, relocation, a child leaving home, or perhaps a developmental step, such as graduation from college. Whatever the precipitating event may be, the person's intense reaction is partly to the present stress but resonates with the earlier unresolved grief.

Normal and Pathological Bereavement

Recent research indicates that only a minority of the bereaved population (about 14 percent) develops intense and enduring pathological grief responses.[11] This research has demonstrated a relationship between pathological grief and the following: *dependent attachment, conflicted attachment, and unexpected loss.* Thus, those who were quite dependent in their relationships with the deceased, those who had conflicted and highly ambivalent relationships with the deceased, and those suffering sudden and unexpected losses should be considered at risk for abnormal grief reactions. Normal and pathological grief reactions can be distinguished on the basis of severity and duration.[12] Thus, in acute grief the bereaved experience all kinds of unsettling and sometimes frightening feelings such as the notion that they are losing their minds as well as somatic symptoms such as headaches and tightness in their chest. All of these reactions are common. If symptoms of acute grief persist for more than six months they may indicate pathological mourning. In general, if overt grief is completely absent, delayed, expressed in a distorted form such as acting out (e.g., abusing alcohol and drugs), or unusually intense or persistent, it indicates that the grieving process has taken an unhealthy form. While the acute symptoms of grief should resolve in the first six months, the total grief process can easily span two to three years. It typically takes longer in children since they can tolerate the feelings of grief for only brief periods and because they need to rework the grief at each developmental phase. No one ever completely recovers from the loss of someone they deeply loved. Recovery from grief means you can face and bear the loss, but you are permanently changed as a result of the experience. Some of these changes may be positive as we may gain or discover strength within ourselves.

Mitigating Factors

A crucial buffering and protective element in facing any stressful life event is a close, stable, and confiding relationship with at least one other person.[13] Whether the bereaved are young or old, men or women, wealthy or impoverished, one major influence in the road to recovery is the ability to make and/or maintain meaningful connections with others. If grievers, because of their pain or lack of social skills or circumstances surrounding the death, isolate themselves from others, then the difficult grief reactions are compounded by loneliness. School-age children may withdraw because of their inability to tolerate the painful grief and their wish not to talk about their loss. The elderly may assume they are a burden and that no one really cares about them. *Whatever the reasoning behind the isolating behavior, helpers can make a significant contribution by facilitating the renewal of social contacts.* In the case of a bereaved person who was a social isolate prior to the loss, the counselor may need to teach social skills, using role-playing and behavior rehearsal techniques. Faulty assumptions need to be challenged and reality tested. Socially withdrawn school-age children will sometimes say that "there is no one in the whole school who isn't a jerk." I respond, "There has to be one kid in your school who is not a jerk. You said there are a thousand students in your school. There has to be one student there who is not a jerk. Find that kid and make friends with him or her."

When working with the bereaved of all ages, you would be well advised to pay close attention to the resources of the person. In the mental health field, it is easy to get caught up in identifying pathology, but in bringing about change you'll get far more leverage from recognizing and highlighting the resources of the person. If you look closely enough you will find them in all individuals no matter how dysfunctional they may be at a given point in time.

It is also worth noting how little help reassurance is to a person in pain. *Reassurance keeps the recipient of the help dependent on the helper.* It is the helper's strength being relied on, e.g., "Don't worry—everything is going to be all right." This may be appropriate in the case of parents talking to small children who are realistically dependent on the adult caretakers in their life. To say the same words to adults, however, is to diminish their abilities to handle their lives. It is far more helpful to notice something about the way the person is coping with the situation that is adaptive and point it out. You might say, for example, "The last time we talked about this, you didn't see any hope whatsoever. Today you have mentioned two alternatives as possible solutions." In this case it is the bereaved individual's strength that is being highlighted and reinforced, not the helper's.

Helping the Bereaved throughout the Life Cycle

While this book focuses much attention on developmental issues that need to be considered in helping the bereaved throughout the life cycle, some guidelines would apply to all ages and stages of development. *First of all, helpers must come to terms with their own anxiety about death.* We cannot expect to be helpful when we ourselves have a need to deny our own mortality or avoid dealing with our own sense of loss or unresolved grief. In fact, if we do not do this work with ourselves we may find ourselves trying to resolve these conflicts through the shared experiences and feelings of those we seek to help. In the field of counseling and psychotherapy in recent decades there has been much healthy attention paid to the issue of countertransference, or the distortions that can arise in our work deriving from our own unresolved issues. No issue is more ripe for countertransference than that of death and dying. Those of us in the caregiving professions are far from being immune to the same kinds of fears, doubts, anxieties, and uncertainties about death that plague the people to whom we extend our help. If this is honestly faced and dealt with in the caregiver's own therapy or supervision and training, it need not be an unhealthy interference in helping others.

Whenever possible, work with the bereaved in the context of their families. So much more can be accomplished by enlisting the natural healing forces that exist within families.

This is especially true when working with bereaved children, but persons of all ages gather strength from the support and concern of their nuclear and extended families. There will occasionally be exceptions to this general guideline; that is, when family relationships are exceptionally destructive and an individual may have appropriately distanced himself from the family for his own emotional well-being. In the vast majority of cases, however, the bereaved will benefit from the helper's orientation toward the family as an ally in healing.

Show utmost respect for the spiritual and religious beliefs, ethnic and cultural heritage of the bereaved. The deeply held values, customs, and beliefs of the bereaved and their families provide much meaning, purpose, and richness to their lives and under no circumstances should the helper call these into question. Studies of childhood bereavement reveal that even young children can endure such potentially upsetting ordeals as an open coffin and kissing the deceased when this is a strongly valued custom in the family and support and encouragement is offered to the child by the family to do so.[14] Our own feelings and values about such customs should not intrude and risk offending the bereaved or their family. Some families sensitively modify their usual mourning customs and rituals to make it easier for a child. In such a case, the counselor might be asked to offer suggestions as to what would be most helpful. The discussions in the subsequent chapters regarding developmental considerations may be useful in providing such recommendations.

Avoid overcatastrophizing. If we expect trauma, especially with children and highly suggestible adolescents, we will get trauma. It is imperative to hold and convey the conviction that the bereaved person will survive the painful grieving experience. We should never assume that a particular death will be traumatic for a person lest it become a self-fulfilling prophecy. Research in resiliency indicates that certain individuals seem to thrive even in the face of very extreme stressful events.[15]

Empathize with the pain of the griever without overidentifying. In order to be helpful in counseling the bereaved we need to be able to put ourselves in the place of grievers and feel their pain without losing our own sense of self. Being able to express empathy for the range of painful feelings experienced by the bereaved will convey acceptance and understanding in a way that enables the mourner to bear these feelings more easily. We must be capable of being deeply moved and affected by the feelings of the griever. We need to be with the bereaved on a feeling level. At the same time we cannot lose our identity in the process. No matter how closely we may share the griever's feelings, we are not the griever. Furthermore, no matter how hard we try we cannot fully share and appreciate the bereaved's feelings because we are different persons. I once knew a minister with a heart of gold. He was a kind and giving man who was well loved. When one of the families in his congregation experienced a death, he would call on them to offer his sympathy. Often the family would end up trying to console him. In spite of the best intentions in the world, he would end up overidentifying with the bereaved and render himself of little help to the family.

You also need to be able to detach in order to maintain objectivity. If you can't express empathy, your responses to the bereaved are likely to be overly intellectualized and emotionally sterile. However, if you are unable to pull back and detach yourself you will lose objectivity. These skills of empathy and detachment and the dynamic interplay between them are regarded as an integral part of all counseling and psychotherapy.[16] Thus, you must be able to strike a balance between empathy with the pain and sufficient detachment to achieve objectivity. One without the other will result in significant obstacles to offering genuine help to the bereaved.

Be sensitive to the external conditions of the griever's life. In the fervor to tackle the grief work, you must be aware of the realistic hardships that the bereaved may be facing in their daily lives. If the death resulted in the loss of the family's primary source of income there may be pressing financial stresses. The family may face the need to relocate. There may be bitter squabbles in the family regarding division of the estate. All of these problems and concerns may leave grievers preoccupied and unable to focus on their inner feelings. This should not be mistaken for resistance to grief counseling, although certainly these realistic concerns could be used in the service of resistance, i.e., avoiding one's grief. Many contemporary students of counseling and psychotherapy regard resistance as frequently stemming from the counselor's reluctance to getting really involved with the patient, or the counselor's pursuing goals in conflict with the true needs of the patient. Thus, resistance is not seen as flowing from the patient, but rather viewed as resulting primarily from errors in the approach of the counselor. One such error would be exclusive focus on the inward feelings of loss, while ignoring the harsh realities the bereaved may be facing in their daily lives.

Structure and create conditions in the counseling so as to elicit verbal expressions of grief. You must repeatedly affirm the value of putting the painful mixture of feelings that constitute grief into words. The bereaved need explicit assurance that it is good for them to do this. So often the mourner gets mixed messages from well-intended, concerned family and friends. Given the strong denial of death in our society and the defenses that are quickly erected by survivors, many times the bereaved get the unmistakable message that they should hide their true feelings lest they be too upsetting for others. The grievers may need to hear directly that you are ready to listen to their real feelings.

With young or nonverbal grievers, stimulate creative productions wherein the feelings of loss can be expressed. Young children, preschool and some of school age, may not be able to express their grief in words. Even some older individuals who are particularly nonverbal may have difficulty putting their grief into words. In this case you need to encourage the expression of feelings through creative productions such as symbolic play with young children, artwork, and drawings, or writing. These interventions will be covered in more detail in subsequent chapters dealing with different stages and developmental issues.

Be more of a guide and companion through the grieving journey, rather than a representative of reality. This point is made by John Bowlby in his writings on helping the bereaved.[17] The bereaved benefit much more from our attentive listening to and understanding of their feelings than from rushing in to correct their distortions of reality. While I believe that there are times when these distortions have to be confronted in order to remove obstacles to the grief work, Bowlby's emphasis on being a guide and companion is very useful especially in the early stages of grief work. To be confrontational in early work with the grieving will surely lead to resistance and not much progress will be made. The way confrontation is done and, of course, its timing will greatly affect the results. More will be said about confrontation skills in the chapters on helping bereaved adults. To work effectively with the bereaved of all ages, counselors need to master the skills of active listening.

Normalize the grief process without appearing insensitive to the pain of the bereaved. You need to help the griever develop appropriate expectations about the length of the grieving process and the wide range of responses that can be considered normal although they may be atypical of the person at any other time.[18] When normalizing the experience of grief, you must be careful not to minimize the feelings of the bereaved individual. Instead of finding your words comforting, grievers may think their feelings are being treated as routine and taken lightly.

Encourage the bereaved to tell their story and to share their memories. When we are in pain we experience a powerful desire to unburden and share our story with someone who will listen and care. Sometimes there is an equally strong fear that if we do so the response of the listener will be disappointing and then we will feel even more alone. You must actively pursue and create opportunities for the mourner to share his story and review the emotionally laden memories of the deceased. Important memories of good times as well as bad times need to be reviewed. This process helps the griever withdraw the emotional investment in the lost loved person, and to resume his involvement with life as fully as possible.

You need to exercise patience that allows for going up and down the "turf" many times until mastery of the painful emotions of grief is achieved. Memories will need to be shared again and again. Stories will need to be told and retold. The griever will need to cry and cry some more. The counselor ideally will convey in his words and actions that all of this is okay. The bereaved need to be encouraged to go as far as they can on any given occasion. When they can't go any further, they need to be told, "It's okay. Perhaps you can go a little further at another time, a time when it will be a little more comfortable for you." You might say to the griever, "You have gone as far as you can for now. It's like taking out a photograph album. You look at the pictures and they bring up lots of feelings. Some are warm, happy feelings as you are reminded of the good times. Then you come to pictures that make you sad or cause you pain. You look at them for a while, and then you decide to put them away and then take them out again at a later time, a time that's more comfortable for you."

Give permission not to grieve. No one can grieve all the time no matter how close the relationship. Nevertheless, mourners may feel guilty about distracting themselves from their grief to do something enjoyable or relaxing. The bereaved should be encouraged to take breaks, to get rest, exercise, to eat properly, in short to go on living. In no way does this indicate that they love the deceased any less. In fact, they can be told that in order to grieve properly they must pace themselves, conserve energy, and take care of themselves.

Assist grievers in anticipating difficult times. A middle-aged widow said, "The first set of holidays you go through after the death, you just simply try to survive!" Anniversaries, birthdays, day of death, and holidays are all potentially very difficult times for the bereaved. Anticipating these times and planning for them allow a sense of personal control and mastery that may enable mourners to cope more effectively.

Help mourners to find a life-enhancing way of honoring the memory of the loved one. Commemoration is the third task of mourning. You can explore with the bereaved the strongly held values of the deceased. The causes that the deceased supported and believed in need to be reviewed. It may give significant meaning and purpose to the life of grievers to dedicate themselves to carrying on some of the unfinished work of the deceased. A young man whose father had died the year before shared his guilt that he had been very critical of his father in his last two visits with him. He blamed his father for the divorce between his parents when he was only seven. Unfortunately, a week after the second of these two highly emotional visits, the father suddenly suffered a fatal heart attack. Exploring with this man in his late twenties the different values and interests of his father revealed that his father had been involved for many years in conservation and environmental causes. He decided that one of the best ways he could honor the memory of his father was to continue the work to which his father had been so committed. Involving himself in environmental projects gave a new sense of meaning and purpose to his life and, in addition, helped to undo the terrible burden of guilt he had carried since his father's death.

For every bereaved individual and family, the manner in which the memory of the loved one can be celebrated and honored will be different. Pursuing this uniqueness and guiding the bereaved to find their own special way can be of enormous consolation.

When the period of acute grief subsides, stimulate and encourage grievers to develop new interests and activities. During the period of acute grief mourners are likely to be so preoccupied with their pain and the pressing details and changes that have to be attended to that they are unlikely to be able to concentrate on anything else. After this very hectic period, around three months after the death, mourners may suddenly find that well-meaning friends and family have resumed their usual tasks and responsibilities and they find themselves very much alone and feeling empty. At this point, encouragement to develop new interests, to participate in new activities, to meet other people and, in general, to begin a new life will be needed.

Help the bereaved to develop a new sense of identity. To the extent that grievers have defined themselves in relation to the deceased and have not developed a strong independent sense of self, they will need much help in developing an identity of their own. Some grievers may have viewed themselves as weak and inadequate in relation to their strong, competent spouses or a child may have felt helpless in relation to a powerful and overly protective parent. When given the proper encouragement many of these grievers may suddenly discover themselves to be a lot stronger and more competent than they ever imagined possible. Others may intensify their bids for others to take care of them and continue to define themselves as helpless and inadequate. You can offer vital encouragement to those struggling to shed faulty and limiting concepts of self and you can be enormously helpful in confronting the self-defeating maneuvers of those who attempt to continue hiding behind their pseudohelplessness. *Research reveals that encouraging the excessively dependent to grieve can actually make things worse.*[19] Typically, they don't need encouragement to grieve since they have grieved intensely already. They do need firm insistence that they are capable of resuming full participation in life and a plan of action to accomplish this in small steps.

Enable mourners to relinquish the old dreams in order to make room for new ones. Tasks 6 and 7 of mourning require letting go and moving on. This can be an exceedingly painful transition. To give up long-cherished hopes and dreams and then to dare to create new ones is one of the hardest tasks that anyone will undertake. You will need to review patiently the old dreams and plans until the emotional investment is gradually relinquished, at which point it becomes possible for the bereaved to entertain new possibilities.

Timing is critical with these interventions. Introducing the idea of making new goals before mourning the lost aspirations and hopes will likely be experienced as insensitivity to the feelings of the griever. Failure to provide a "gentle push" when the bereaved are ready to move on may be experienced as desertion. It is vital to listen to the feelings behind the words so that we can really hear the messages of those we seek to help.

Summary

Throughout the life cycle we are faced with losses and the need to grieve. If we fail to mourn, the grief is likely to be expressed in a delayed or distorted form. Even very young children can be helped to grieve although they will do so in a different way than adults. Seven tasks of mourning were delineated in this chapter. In addition, guidelines applicable to all stages of the life cycle were discussed. In the following six chapters bereavement at different stages of the life cycle—preschool, school-age, adolescent, young adult, midlife, and the elderly—will be examined in relation to special losses. Developmental considerations as well as practical guidelines for intervention will be presented.

2

Helping Preschool Children to Grieve

Adults wish to spare children the difficulty of going through the painful grieving process. It is the defense of magical thinking: "If we don't talk about it, maybe it never happened." Often parents of young children say that their preschool children aren't affected by a loss in the family because "they are too young to understand." Young children are even quite capable of anticipating loss. One of my early experiences in private practice was being consulted by a young couple with a two-and-a-half-year-old boy, Robert, who would not sleep at night. The parents had tried everything. They had allowed Robert to sleep in their bed. The mother tried sleeping with Robert in his bed. The mother also tried sleeping with him on the couch downstairs. But nothing would console Robert who would scream for hours before finally falling to sleep out of sheer exhaustion. I asked this couple if there were any tensions between them that could be threatening to the child. Both of them adamantly denied any such thing. At the next visit the mother showed up alone. She tearfully explained that her husband had told her that for some time he had been having an affair and was planning to leave her and did so that week. This toddler was reacting quite emotionally to something that the parents were unable to confront openly with each other and was in a stage of anticipatory grief consisting of a vigorous protest against the sensed loss.

Children Need Simple and Honest Explanations

Most parents would not take their preschool children to the pediatrician without some explanation of why they are going, e.g., that they have a cold or sore throat and need some medicine. Parents, however, will rationalize to themselves that preschoolers need no explanation when a parent dies or the parents decide to separate because "they're too young to understand." Even worse is the attempt to deceive preschoolers in order to present a more palatable reality. Children can bear the truth, no matter how painful, much more easily than they can handle being deceived. The view that preschoolers (with the exception of preverbal children) are too young to understand stems primarily from the need of the parents to avoid the pain involved in confronting their preschoolers about harsh realities. Children (from the age of toddlers on) need a simple, direct, and honest explanation from the adults in their lives, whom they rely on and need to believe in. This is especially true at a time of family trauma.

Myths about Childhood Grief

British psychiatrists and researchers have written extensively about the capacity of very young children, including the infant and toddler, to grieve for their mothers when separated.[1] The immediate response is one of shock and numbness. The initial shock is followed by vigorous protest, loud and persistent crying, and motoric agitation, as children desperately search for the missing mother. This protest stage is followed by despair, during which time children become apathetic and withdrawn. Finally, children manifest detachment whereby they insulate themselves from feelings so as not to be hurt or disappointed again.

The British investigators have challenged a number of common myths about childhood grief including the notion that young children soon forget about the lost mother and that grief in childhood is of brief duration. John Bowlby has demonstrated in his studies that, in fact, the longing and yearning for the lost mother persists for quite some time in addition to search behavior as children attempt to find the lost parent. It is easy to mistake the denial that follows the intensely painful periods of protest and despair as evidence that children have forgotten the loss, when in reality they have simply distanced themselves from their intensely painful feeling state.

Developmental Considerations: Infants

The capacity to grieve will certainly vary according to age, developmental level, and the circumstances surrounding the loss. According to researchers the capacity to tolerate longing and yearning for the deceased loved one increases with age.

The verbal capacity in the infant to assimilate a loss is obviously not developed. If a baby's mother dies in the first six months of its life, the infant may exhibit significant distress. The infant has experienced the mother as an extension of self with no clear distinction between self and other. Later, in the second half of the first year, the infant becomes more aware of the differentiation between self and other but sees the mother as primarily existing to meet its needs. Beginning with the second year of life, the baby becomes interested in the mother as a person in her own right. In this early preverbal stage of development in Western culture, it is usually the mother who is the central figure in the life of the infant. The father will play crucial roles later in development. Loss of the mother during the first year of life through separation, death, or abandonment potentially can impair the child's development of what Erik Erikson called *basic trust.*[2] This is a sense of optimism and confidence acquired by the infant as a result of sensitive and caring parental responses to the infant's needs.

Developmental Considerations: Toddlers

Children under two are thought to have little concept of death. With the development of language, however, children begin to express curiosity about all aspects of their world and can be expected to have questions and concerns about death.

Until infants reach the stage of object permanence that occurs around age one, each time the mother leaves, the infant fears she is gone forever. These fears of abandonment are allayed by the mother's frequent returns and soothing and comforting responses that eventually greatly reduce these terrors. Upon reaching the stage of object permanence a baby has mastered the concept that mother exists even when out of sight and not immediately available to the infant. Obviously, the death of the mother before the baby has reached one year may delay the achievement of object permanence. So, all young children who are beginning to grapple with the mysteries of death have had prior experience with feelings of separation and abandonment to one degree or another.

Toddlers begin around eighteen months to exert a sense of independence. With the increased mobility provided by their rapidly developing motor skills, they begin to separate from mother to explore their environment. They return to mother frequently for emotional "refueling." Fathers also play a crucial role by encouraging the emerging autonomy in toddlers as they move away in tentative steps from the close dependence on mother. This developmental process is frequently referred to as the separation-individuation phase. If either parent should die during this phase, the toddler's efforts to achieve autonomy will be significantly hampered.

When toddlers begin to ask questions about death, they should be given simple and direct explanations. They are not capable of comprehending the abstract theological or philosophical aspects of death, but they can be helped to understand that everyone living eventually dies, usually after a long and full life. They can be told when people die their body totally stops working.

Parents should fully utilize the opportunities afforded to teach toddlers about death by capitalizing on their natural curiosity. They will have questions about dead insects or birds. In order to treat the subject of death as a natural part of life and as basic to all living things as birth and growing older, we have to come to terms with our own anxiety about this issue. In his book, *The Denial of Death,* Ernest Becker detailed the many ways in which people avoid awareness of death.[3] Becker viewed this denial of death as having a crippling effect emotionally in that people unable to confront their own death are unable to appreciate life and live fully. The earlier and more naturally the concept of death is taught the more likely children will develop a healthy and fuller appreciation of life.

Many of the guidelines and suggestions offered in this chapter for helping preschool children understand and deal with death are primarily intended for parents and family members. As a caregiver, you are likely to be consulted by parents who are seeking advice on how to answer the questions of their young children about death or how to assist them in grieving. Thus, the practical guidelines to follow are meant to increase your effectiveness as a consultant to the family.

Guidelines for Helping Infants and Toddlers to Grieve

When the mother of an infant dies, the father and adult members of the extended family should do everything possible to arrange for substitute maternal care with the least possible disruption. This is a difficult task for the surviving adult family members because they have their own grief to resolve. The major contribution that helping professionals can make in such cases is to assist the surviving family members in resolving their grief as fully as possible so that continuity of care for the infant can be provided.

When told of a death in their family children in the toddler stage need to be offered both verbal and nonverbal support. They are in the early stages of developing language ability and need a simple and honest explanation of what has happened. They need verbal reassurance that they will be taken care of and nonverbal support in the form of holding, hugs, and the physical presence of caring adults. When the young child is first told about a loss in the family, it can be enormously comforting and supportive to assemble adult family members, including grandparents, on whom the child can rely for continuing nurturance and protection.

A two-and-a-half-year-old, for example, whose mother has been killed in a car accident can be told in the presence of the surviving family the following: "We have something very, very sad to tell you. I want to hold you and have you sit here in my lap along with Grandpa and Grandma and your brothers and sisters because Mommy was badly hurt. She was hurt too badly to live. Her body has stopped working. Mommy has died. She will not be coming back. We will all miss her very, very much, but Daddy is here, Grandma and Grandpa are here, your brothers and sisters are here, and we all love you very much and we will take care of you."

Developmental Considerations: Ages 3–6

This crucial period of development has been described as the *magic years* by Selma Fraiberg.[4] Children in this age range are actively engaged in discovering a larger world beyond their nuclear family. They are absorbed in play, adventurous exploration, and fantasy. They are in competition with their same sex parent and constantly trying out "what the grown-ups do" in their play and fantasy. They play ship captain, police sergeant, nurse, father, mother, and teacher. They feel omnipotent and magical in that they believe that their thoughts about an event can cause it to happen, thus the term the "magic years." If they get angry at the parent and then the parent dies, in their egocentric way of thinking they believe they have caused it. Children of this age need a great deal of help in differentiating the true versus the fantasy causes of events, especially painful ones in their lives. Older preschool children are capable of a greater verbal exchange regarding death than toddlers. They will have many more questions and will need more detailed answers.

It is an age of much guilt. Freud discussed Oedipal conflicts during this age as stemming from the rivalrous feelings of the child toward the same-sex parent for the affections of the opposite-sex parent. If either parent should die during this period the child may assume a double burden of guilt because he may feel that his "wrong" feelings and thoughts caused the death and he must be a "bad" person for having them in the first place. In addition, the death of the same-sex parent during this stage may make it more difficult for the child to solidify his sex role identity through identification with the same-sex parent. Also, feelings of rivalry and competition with siblings for the affections of the parents, so intense at this stage of development, would also leave the child feeling both responsible and intrinsically "bad" should a sibling die during this period.

Guidelines for Helping the Older Preschool Child to Grieve

Take full advantage of opportunities such as the death of a pet to teach the preschool child about death. The preschool child is helped immeasurably in preparing for facing the death of a family member by being allowed to participate fully in mourning the death of a pet. Children who have lost a cat or dog or even a goldfish and have been allowed to view and perhaps even touch and hold the cold, stiff body and participate in the burial as well as a "funeral" can more easily come to a realistic concept of death. I can vividly remember visiting my grandparents at their farm when I was around five. While there one of the young lambs died. My cousins and I decided that nothing but a full-fledged funeral would do. I conducted the service and some of my cousins sang hymns and then we had a procession to the grave with the lamb carried in a cardboard box to its final resting place. A very crude approximation of a cross was placed on the grave. While the grown-ups must have thought this whole thing was pretty silly, it was for me and my cousins one of our first concrete exposures to death and a beginning attempt to make the mysteries of death more comprehensible and less frightening.

Assist preschool children in identifying and expressing their feelings. This is the second task of grieving at all ages (with the exception of the preverbal child). Walter Bonime, a noted analyst, explains that "feelings don't occur in single notes but in chords."[5] When someone we love dies we are sad and this may be our predominant feeling, but it is far from being our only feeling. Those who are grieving often need help in identifying and expressing their other feelings. Especially is this true for the preschool child.

One important source of help for preschool children is for parents to model the expression of these feelings. A parent might say, "I feel terribly sad because I miss your Mommy so much, and it really helps to tell someone how I feel." If the children do not respond with feelings of their own it might be helpful to say, "I bet you feel really sad too." If the children still do not respond the parent could do a monologue about feelings such as, "Most little boys and girls feel really sad when someone in the family dies. They miss their mother so much and wish she could come back but she can't because she is dead and when people die they don't come back. Many times children also feel angry. They feel really mad that this has happened. They ask, 'Why did my mommy have to die; it's not fair!' 'Other kids have a mommy—why couldn't their mommy die?' Sometimes they feel that maybe they did something wrong. "What did I do?" "Maybe it was my fault that this happened!" "Maybe I am being punished!" They might remember a time when they felt angry at their mommy and wished their mommy would die. Then when it happens they think it was their fault. *But angry thoughts and feelings can't cause people to die.* Lots of times kids feel badly because there is nothing that they can do to bring their mommy back. They want so badly to do something. They might even try to look for her but when a person dies they don't come back. That is why we all feel so sad."

At the end of the above monologue it would be good to remind children again that those remaining in the family will continue to be available to them. Some parents may think it strange that this amount of discussion is being recommended for children so young. Studies and clinical experience, however, reveal that in the play of preschool children some very distorted and often scary notions of death emerge as play themes even with children who have never encountered death within their family. These children are already wrestling with their fears and fantasies about death. Therefore the issue becomes whether to abandon them to struggle alone with these distorted notions or to begin the process of helping them develop a realistic understanding of death.

Respect the family's religious beliefs. The religious beliefs of the family and their views of an afterlife will determine what will be explained to the child. If consistent with the family's spiritual faith, the child can be told, "When people die their body totally stops working and is buried in the ground, but their soul goes to a special place that God has created called heaven. So Mommy is with God. She is in a good place and you don't have to worry about her because God takes care of her and watches out for her." Families who do not sincerely hold religious beliefs regarding an afterlife would do well not to offer the comfort of such a concept. Explaining to a young child the idea of a soul going to be with God while the body remains in the ground is difficult enough when this is in keeping with your strong convictions. To explain this to a child when you don't believe it yourself will only result in greater anxiety and confusion in the child who will surely sense your insincerity and doubt. For the families who are unclear about their beliefs the child can be told, "We don't know exactly what happens after a person dies. We know that the body is buried in the ground or exposed to heat and turned to ashes. Many people believe that God has created a special place called heaven where the soul or the personality of the person goes to rest in peace."

Whatever the spiritual beliefs within the family, it is very important that the child realize the family member has died, the body has been placed in the ground or turned to ashes and the person will not be coming back. It is also crucial to make clear to children that the surviving family will continue to take care of them. It is helpful to be very concrete and to state exactly what the arrangements will be. It can be explained, for example, "You will continue to sleep in your same room. We will still eat dinner together but Dad or Grandma will do the cooking." It is important to convey to children at all developmental stages that thoughtful adults are planning for their needs and welfare. This will impart a much-needed sense of security in the midst of loss and family sorrow.

Avoid these common mistakes in explaining death to preschool children. The task of talking to children about death is difficult enough, but when it is done at a time of acute grief for the family it is especially hard. Because mistakes are an inevitable part of parenting, I frequently say to parents that their imperfections and honest acknowledgment of mistakes are a very great favor to their child because they relieve the child from the oppressive burden of having to be perfect. It is important, however, that we learn from our mistakes; thus, we should be aware of some of the common mistakes that can be made when talking to children about a death in the family.[6]

One frequently made mistake is to *describe death to children as "Mommy or Daddy has gone to sleep."* Consequently, children may be frightened for a long time about going to sleep at night for fear that they will not wake up. A similar mistake can be made by *indicating to children that the family member died because he/she was sick.* This can have the unintended effect of leaving children fearful of ever again becoming sick with even a common cold. Instead, children might be told: "Most people get sick many times and get well again, but sometimes people get very sick or sick for a very long time and the body completely wears out and the person dies. But a healthy little boy/girl like you should live a long, long time."

Or, in case of an accident, it might be explained that the family member was hurt very badly and the doctors were not able to keep his/her body working. The parent can explain that most of the time when we get hurt we are able to heal and get well again. It may be comforting to children to remind them of when they had been hurt in some minor way and were able to recover fully as a way of emphasizing the point that most injuries don't result in death.

Another mistake would be to imply that *going to the hospital resulted in the death,* which children might assume if told: "Mommy got sick and went to the hospital and she died." Then, of course, children would be unduly frightened about any subsequent trip to the hospital for them or any other member of the family. Likewise, any discussion of surgery should be handled carefully so as not to *leave the impression the surgery caused the death.*

Finally, there are serious drawbacks *to explaining the death in terms of morality.* To say to children, for example, "God took Daddy to heaven because he was such a good person," may lead children to be fearful that by being either "good" or "bad" they will risk untimely death.

Remember that children often benefit from participation in the funeral. Many children are helped to deal with the unreality of a death in the family by viewing the body, attending the funeral, and going to the grave. All of these experiences help to concretize the death and make it more real. This is the first task of mourning since it is impossible to grieve for a loss that is unreal to us. Whether preschool children should attend the funeral is a judgment call that only the parents can make. Young children who would find it extremely difficult to sit still during the services might be better off with a trusted friend or close relative, thus allowing the rest of the family to participate more fully in the funeral. Children should certainly not be pressured into attending these mourning rituals if they are frightened and strongly protest. At a later time they may be able to visit the grave.

For many children, as with adults, the visit to the grave represents an important milestone in terms of comprehending the reality of the loss. While preschool children should not be forced into attending the funeral or visiting the grave, a "gentle push" or mild encouragement may be helpful. All children may be frightened about the funeral service and the visit to the grave to some extent. If it appears that encouragement and reassurance from the adult are all that's needed to get children over this hurdle then a gentle push is in order.

By temperament some children tend to be fearful of new experiences and need encouragement before undertaking anything unknown. Thus, a judgment needs to be made as to whether the reluctance is in keeping with this temperament pattern or whether it represents a more extreme reaction that calls for a different kind of response.

The parent may test to determine which way to respond by offering mild encouragement such as, "I think it would be helpful for you to go to the funeral. We'll all be together and you can sit by me." If the children still seem unsure more encouragement can be offered. If they seem genuinely frightened then it would be appropriate to skip the funeral. If children are able to go they may benefit from the outpouring of affection and support offered to the family, and from the sense of participation in the mourning rituals that represents such a significant event in the life of a family.

Be sensitive to the special feelings and conflicts stirred in the preschooler by the death of a sibling. Although the concentration in this chapter is on the impact of the death of a parent on the preschooler, the death of a sibling can also be devastating. Preschoolers may experience quite painfully the loss of a loved constant companion and playmate. If the death of the sibling leaves them as the only child, their loneliness may be especially acute. They may also feel frightened that their parents may die too, leaving them totally alone in the world. Preschoolers may manifest regressive behavior such as loss of previously established urinary or bowel control or may suddenly resort to baby talk. They sometimes develop somatic symptoms resembling those manifested by the dead brother or sister during the terminal illness. Sleep difficulties are common following the death of a sibling in this age group. In addition to their intense sadness and fear they may feel anger at all the attention commanded by a dying brother or sister. These resentments may trigger much guilt after the death along with the expectation of punishment for having such bad thoughts. As previously mentioned they may even feel that they caused the death, especially in the "magic years." Often there is an upsurge of separation anxiety with the surviving children in fear of being left alone. These fears may actually be compounded by the natural tendency of the parents to overprotect the surviving children, especially the very young. Preschoolers in addition to their own pain are deeply affected by the severe emotional distress of their parents at the time of death of a brother or sister.

The death of grandparents can also profoundly affect preschoolers. Grandparents can be very important loving, nurturing, and protective figures in the lives of young children. While their death rarely threatens continuity of care as does the death of a parent, the impact can be enormous. Obviously, the degree of emotional closeness between the child and the grandparent will greatly affect the course bereavement will take. As with other deaths in the family, the degree of parental distress will also be an important factor. The loss may be especially acute where the grandparent has lived with the family or been a primary caretaker. For many children grandparents play a special role even if the contact is limited by geographical distance or other constraints. The loss of grandparents along with the death of family pets are the most frequent deaths to be faced by preschool children.

Useful Ways to Talk to Preschool Children about Death

Metaphors

In explaining to preschool children a concept as bewildering as death, the use of metaphors can be effective. Rabbi Earl Grollman has used the metaphor of *a flower that blooms and then withers and finally dies but we are able to remember how beautiful it was.*[7] A metaphor I have used frequently with young children in discussing death is "The Trees in the Forest." I explain, "As part of the natural growth and development of the forest some of the older trees, especially those that have been sick for a long time with some kind of serious disease, must die in order to make way for the young trees. The young trees then have enough sunshine and food to continue growing." In the case of sudden death or death of a young person, it can be added, "It is usually the case in the forests that only the old and the diseased trees die but occasionally there will be a violent storm with wind and lightning that will bring down even a young strong tree. Sometimes things like that happen in life too. It is usually the old and those who have been sick for a very long time with some kind of very serious sickness who die. Occasionally, however, young people die as a result of accidents that lead to very serious injuries and cause the body of even a young strong person to totally stop working." An excellent book on metaphors is entitled *Therapeutic Metaphors for Children and the Child Within* by Joyce Mills and Richard Crowley.[8]

Story Telling

Another useful way of talking with preschool children about death is through story telling. Children are typically fascinated by stories and it is possible to impart a great deal of learning in a nonthreatening way through the use of stories. Most stories, as well as metaphors, have the advantage of providing some distance from the everyday situation of children; this allows children to listen and to be affected in a meaningful way because they do not feel anxious.

A story told by Joyce Mills, for example, is "The Three-Legged Dog":

Last week as I was driving down the street with my ten-year-old son Casey he suddenly said, "Mom, look over there!" He pointed excitedly to the left. "It's a three-legged dog!" he exclaimed in amazement.

"Yes." I said, "that's a three-legged dog all right."

"But, Mom," he protested, "look at what she's doing! She's playing ball, she's running, she's sitting, she's eating her bone. She's doing everything our dog does, but she has only three legs. How is that possible?"

Casey continued to question me curiously. "But Mom, how can she do all those things?"

"Well, Casey," I answered, "I guess she learned how to adjust to not having that other leg, that fourth leg. I guess she learned how to have fun with the three legs that were left."

Again Casey questioned, "But don't you think that was hard to do?"

"Yes," I said, "probably in the beginning it was hard. It takes all of us a little time to learn something new. But once we learn it, that new learning is forever."

After a while Casey asked what had happened to the dog's fourth leg. I said I didn't know for sure—maybe she had been born that way, maybe she lost it as a pup, maybe she lost it recently. It didn't really matter. What mattered, I told him, was that the dog had lost something important and then learned how to use what remained in a new way.

Casey liked my answer and sat back comfortably in the car for the rest of the drive home. When he got home, he ran to tell his friend all about the amazing, three-legged dog.[9]

This beautiful story could be used with a family suffering a loss of a parent through divorce or death. The story suggests the ability of the individual or family to organize in a new way and to make use of existing strengths and resources in facing adversity. This is an extremely important message to convey to children at the time of loss. They need to have the opportunity to express their sadness and all their other feelings, but they also need to be brought in touch with existing resources, both within themselves and within the family, to cope with and survive the loss.

A story I've created for young children is intended to highlight these resources:

> Little Johnny Rabbit was playing with his fellow rabbits in his neighbor's yard when he noticed a big commotion at his house. All the mother and father rabbits in the neighborhood were coming out of his house and he saw his mother on the porch crying.
>
> Johnny started to run toward his mother when one of his buddies, Frankie, headed him off and said, "Your father is dead."
>
> Johnny said, "No! No! It's not true! Why do you tell me such a terrible lie? It can't be true."
>
> "It is true," said his friend Frankie. "That's why your mom is crying and so many people are coming to your house."
>
> Johnny went racing toward his mother screaming, "It's not true! It's not true!"
>
> When he reached his mother she hugged him and held him for a long time and then she said, "It is true, Johnny. Your daddy has died and we are all very sad."
>
> Johnny didn't want to make his mother more sad so he quietly slipped away and went to a hiding place that only he knew about and he cried and cried. Never before had he cried so hard and so long. He felt very sad. He also felt scared. How are we going to get along without Daddy, he wondered? "It won't be the same without him." He also felt angry. "Why did this have to happen? Why did it have to be my daddy?"

"Why couldn't it be somebody else's daddy? Daddy was so good. Why couldn't it have happened to somebody mean?"

Then Johnny began to think that maybe it was his fault. Maybe he had been bad and this was his punishment. Then he had the thought, "If I were to be really, really good from now on maybe my daddy could come back."

As he was thinking all of these things and feeling so down, a very wise old rabbit by the name of Uncle Harry came along. Uncle Harry saw Johnny crying and began to speak to him. "I know that you must feel so sad because you really miss your father. We all loved him." Johnny continued to cry and then he told Uncle Harry about his feelings. Uncle Harry listened patiently as Johnny described his sadness, his anger, his wishes that his father would come back, and his feeling that it was his fault. He told Uncle Harry about his idea that if he were extra good maybe his daddy would come back.

As he told these things to Uncle Harry, Johnny discovered how much better it felt to share his feelings with someone he trusted and someone he knew would understand. Uncle Harry said to Johnny, "I have listened to many young rabbits who have lost someone they loved through death. They too have talked about their sadness, about their missing their loved one and wishing that rabbit could come back. They, too, talked about blaming themselves and thinking that if they were good the one they loved might come back." When Uncle Harry said these things, Johnny no longer felt quite so alone in his feelings. Other rabbits have felt the same way, he thought to himself.

Uncle Harry said, "When someone dies they are dead. When you are dead you do not come back. Your life is over and your body is buried in the ground but all of those who are left behind and who loved that rabbit will remember all the beautiful and good things about his life. In this way we can continue to feel close to the one who has died."

Uncle Harry continued, "Not all of your memories will be happy. You may remember some times when you did things that made your father angry with you or he did things that made you angry with him, but this did not cause him to die nor will being good bring him back. It has nothing to do with being good or bad."

Uncle Harry explained, "We die when our bodies completely stop working because of old age or because of very serious sickness or accidents where we are hurt so badly that our bodies can't keep working. Most rabbits live a long, long time and a healthy young rabbit like you should too."

Uncle Harry added, "You have many good memories of your father. That will help you in many situations because you have learned much from him. Just like your father, you have many friends and your mother and a brother and a sister, so you are not alone. I will be glad to help too in any way I can. So together we will make it through this." Although Johnny still felt very sad, he realized that he was not alone. Uncle Harry said, "Let's go back to the house now." So hand in hand Uncle Harry and Johnny walked slowly back home.

Monologues about Other Children's Feelings

In addition to direct modeling, adults can be helpful particularly with inhibited and reticient children who have trouble verbalizing any feelings by discussing "other children" who have gone through the same thing. Such a monologue might go as follows: "Other three-year-olds, when their mommy died, have talked about how very sad they felt. Sometimes they felt they did something wrong and that this was why their mommy died. Maybe they got mad at their mommy and said, 'I wish you were dead.' Then their mommy got really sick and died, so they thought it was their fault. But their mommy didn't die because they got mad at her. All children get mad at their mommies and all mommies get mad at their children, even though they love each other very much, but that doesn't cause anybody to die. What causes people to die is very, very serious and long sickness that causes the body to totally stop working. When people die they don't move, and they don't feel anything. Sometimes people will have very serious accidents that cause them to be hurt so badly, their body stops working. But most people live a very long time and a strong, healthy, young child like you should live a long, long time."

Additional Strategies to Help Preschoolers Grieve

Mastery through Play

Many young children will work out their sense of loss and pain through play. Play is the natural mode of expression for young children and a primary method of relieving emotional distress. Through their play they have the opportunity to rework experiences that were too painful or overwhelming.

Young children who have experienced death in the family may play funeral or repeatedly bury dolls or play objects in an attempt to master their fears and other painful feelings. Through their play children attempt actively to master what was passively experienced and was overwhelming to their developing ego at the time. Parents should not be alarmed by the child's play and in fact should view it as an adaptive effort on the part of the child to come to terms with his feelings. Preschool children may also express their emotional distress following the death of a family member through drawings, artwork, and clay productions. Signs of post-traumatic play and the therapeutic use of play will be discussed later in this chapter.

Modeling Defenses

Some children at this age have not developed adequate defensive resources and are overwhelmed by their feelings. Even children with adequate defenses may have moments when they feel overwhelmed by their intense feelings of sadness, anger, guilt, fear, or combinations of these emotions. What can the parent or counselor do at these times? They can model their own use of defenses. They might say, "When I feel so sad I can't stand it anymore, I might turn the TV on and watch a funny show like Bill Cosby and that gets my mind off it." Or they might say, "If I get really mad and I want to feel better, sometimes it helps a lot if I sit down and draw something, it takes my mind off it." The adult might try to elicit from children some ideas of their own about what could make them feel better and encourage them and reinforce them for trying these activities. If children are unable to come up with anything, the parent or counselor may be able to suggest activities based on their knowledge of the interests and preferences of the children.

Highlighting the Child's Strength and Inner Resources

The natural coping styles and strategies that children have developed for handling difficult experiences should be identified, highlighted, and reinforced. Parents as well as counselors trying to help children resolve painful life experiences would be well advised to take inventory of the child's strengths and natural ways of handling stress. Some children may rely primarily on distraction and when they become anxious will simply drop what they are doing and turn to something else. Other children ask for a hug while still others may be able to talk about what they are feeling. Others may work it out through their play or drawings or fantasy. Still others may get angry and blame others for their distress. All of these are ways of handling anxiety and stress. These styles of coping represent existing resources in the child to be encouraged and built upon. Such an approach was used by Micky's mother after the death of his father. Micky, a four-year-old, would immediately leave the room or go play in a corner whenever his father was mentioned. Sensitive to his need to deny his overwhelming feelings, his mother bolstered his defenses by stating, "It is good that you know how to go play and think about other things when you are too upset to think about your father." William Van Ornum and John Mordock discuss these ego supportive strategies in depth in their book, *Crisis Counseling with Children and Adolescents.*[10]

When to Refer for Psychotherapy

In her studies of children who had lost a parent Erna Furman found that the continuing availability of the surviving parents was especially helpful in enabling children to cope.[11] This is especially important with the preschool child who is still quite dependent and vulnerable. Also helpful, according to Furman, are familiar surroundings and the presence of other family members. A number of authors have stressed the importance of one consistent parent substitute to provide daily care for the young child whose parent dies. But Furman stresses that, even in those fortunate circumstances where there is a parent substitute, the child is still not spared the pain and distress of mourning. The care and support of the remaining family helps the child to do the grief work. The modeling of mourning by the surviving parent is a crucial influence especially with the young child.

Some parents may simply be too grief-stricken themselves to be effective in assisting or guiding their child. The death of a parent, no matter how well handled by the surviving parent, may be traumatic for some children. When either of these conditions exists, referral for psychotherapy is appropriate.

Therapy might focus on helping the surviving parent work through his/her grief so that the parent could then assist the children in coping with their sorrow. Alternatively, the children might be seen for the purpose of directly facilitating their grief work. In many cases, both of these goals would become central to the psychotherapeutic intervention.

Post-traumatic Stress Disorder

While the magnitude of loss is huge when a parent of young children dies, we ought not to assume it will be traumatizing. It is normal and common for young children to react intensely to a death in a family. Regressive behavior including a return to bed-wetting, increased thumb sucking, and baby talk occur frequently. Sleep difficulties and separation fears often increase for a while after a death. In some cases, the preschooler may develop somatic symptoms resembling those that preceded the death of a parent or a sibling and may well reflect their fear that they will suffer the same fate. For most young children it will undoubtedly be an extremely painful and stressful time, but it need not arrest the growth and development of their personality. This chapter has suggested a number of ways that parents and counselors can help young children so that damaging effects are prevented. Yet there are many other variables that determine the impact of such a stressful event on the life of a preschooler. Among the factors beyond the control of the surviving parent are temperament patterns in the child present from birith, the circumstances surrounding the death, and the relationship between the child and the deceased parent.

How can the parent or counselor know if the impact on particular children is traumatic? In recent years much attention has been given in the mental health profession to a syndrome known as post-traumatic stress disorder. This disorder can be caused by an event outside the usual range of human experience that is extremely stressful. Certainly the death of a parent for preschool children would fall into this category. But, again, it needs to be emphasized that it is not necessarily traumatic.

Some of the common manifestations of this syndrome are recurrent and frightening dreams related to the traumatic event. Repetitive and intrusive recollections of the stressful event are also common. Also typical are exaggerated startle responses to loud noises or sudden movement. A general state of hypervigilance is often seen as if the person were expecting additional trauma and therefore needs to be constantly on guard. These kinds of symptoms have frequently been observed in adults and children alike who have experienced an unusually stressful event in their lives. In some cases time may prove to be an important ally in the healing process, but it is not always enough; psychotherapy may be needed. Certainly, if these symptoms persist past six months after the death of the parent, a consultation with a qualified child therapist should be arranged.

Post-traumatic Play

Since preschool children often give expression to their emotional distress through their play, additional clues regarding possible traumatization may be gathered through careful observation of their free play. Lenore Terr is a child psychiatrist who has studied extensively the play of children who have been traumatized.[12] She worked with twenty-three children who were victims of the Chowchilla schoolbus kidnapping incident. These children were taken at gunpoint, held in pitch-dark vans for eleven hours, and kept in an underground burial place for another sixteen hours. As a result of her studies of these victims and children who had been traumatized by other harsh experiences, she developed a description of the characteristics of post-traumatic play.

One feature that she noted is compulsive repetitiveness—i.e., the play tends to be repeated over and over in a compulsive, driven manner. It is almost as if the child has little choice but to continue to repeat this form of play. The driving force behind it relates to Freud's concept of repetition compulsion, the tendency to repeat or recreate the traumatic situation in a belated attempt to master it. It is believed that anxiety underlies this form of play and that the child attempts to master his anxiety by re-creating in his play the traumatic situation.

Another characteristic delineated by Terr is the literalness of the play. The play lacks the usual imaginative qualities typical of preschool children. It is, rather, a transparent or very thinly disguised repetition of the painful experience. So, for example, children who have lost a father in an accident may in their play repetitively create accidents and bring people to the hospital where they die and are magically brought back to life. Alternatively, the children may have rescue vehicles and personnel at the scene of the accident who are able to save the person; or, perhaps, the children will invoke the powers of superheroes who prevent the accident from happening altogether. All of these variations are attempts to rework the overwhelming traumatic experience so that the child can gain a sense of mastery and control over events that have left him feeling so utterly helpless and powerless. This sense of personal control is crucial to mental health.

Another characteristic of posttraumatic play identified by Terr is the failure of the play to relieve anxiety. Whereas the play of young children typically relieves their emotional distress, in the case of traumatic experiences it takes many repetitions over a period of time to achieve a sense of mastery and control. Sometimes assistance is needed from trained child therapists in order to resolve the underlying feelings that have been so overpowering.

The Therapeutic Use of Fantasy Play

While the therapeutic use of the preschool child's play may be a primary mode of intervention by the child therapist, the surviving parent and other family members need to be brought in as active participants and collaborators. The role of the parent(s) was crucial to the outcome in the following case examples:

Michele was five when seen in individual play sessions. She had been referred as a result of extreme anxiety that made it difficult for her to sit still and adjust to her kindergarten class. When Michele was three and a half her father had been shot and killed in his office during a robbery. In Michele's play, she frequently created scenes where one catastrophe after another would occur. Typically, someone would die or be murdered. Sometimes tall buildings would come crashing down and entire cities would be crushed.

These play scenarios were suggestive of the devastating impact the murder of her father had on the family. Sometimes she would laugh during the midst of the catastrophic happenings in an obvious attempt to deny her anxiety. Sometimes these catastrophes were undone by powerful superheroes. Her sense of vulnerability and fears of making new attachments were vividly expressed in one session, when in the midst of play, she turned to me abruptly and asked, "Do you think someone could break in here and kill you?" Gradually, Michele was able to work through her fears and intense rage regarding the loss of her father through the safe distance provided by the fantasy play. She was eventually able to talk more directly about her feelings regarding the murder of her father and her anxiety greatly subsided. Her mother actively participated in the therapy and also joined a bereavement group that enabled her to complete her grief work. Thus, her mother's recovery from grief served as a powerful role model for Michele.

Jason was seen in play therapy at the age of four after his two-year-old sister had died following a brief illness. Over and over Jason played with the ambulance and hospital as one person after another fell sick and needed to make a quick trip to the hospital. Jason had been acting out at home by being very oppositional, provocative, and prone to severe temper outbursts. His parents noted that he seemed to be much calmer after being punished. Jason was experiencing guilt regarding his sister's death and was actively seeking punishment to alleviate these feelings. Eventually, he was able to tell me about a time when he got really angry with his sister and shouted at her, "I wish you were never born!" Directly at that time and in the course of many subsequent play scenes, I was able to reinforce with him over and over that "angry words and thoughts don't cause people to die." His parents were advised to look for opportunities to reinforce this at home as well, which they did repeatedly. Gradually, he would say this to himself as he was taking people to the hospital in his play scenarios. Finally, the play with hospitals and ambulances stopped altogether.

Through the use of symbolic play he was able to work through the guilt and give up the distorted notion that he was able to cause magically the death of his sister by virtue of his angry feelings toward her. His acting-out behavior at home also subsided. Once again, his family played an active role in the counseling and in bringing about a resolution.

Summary

Death in the family, and especially the death of a parent, is an event of enormous magnitude in the life of preschool children. But we need not conclude that it will inevitably be traumatic. This chapter has outlined some of the important things that parents, counselors, and other helpers can do to facilitate the child's grieving and provide the kind of stable and caring environment that is so essential at a time of significant loss. It has been emphasized in this chapter that surviving parents and other family members are called upon to provide this vital help and support at a time when they are acutely suffering their own grief. One of the most meaningful contributions that friends, community, and professional helpers can make is to support the surviving family as they attend to the grief work of each of its remaining members.

3

Helping School-Age Children to Grieve

School-age children are much more able than younger children to share their grief. Patty's mother died when she was ten. Patty was able to put her longing into words while remembering her mother's ability to make every family occasion special. She described all the baking and decorating her mother would do around the holidays and how she made a big fuss over everyone's birthday. With tears and much sadness she described how empty everyone now feels in the family around the holidays even though everyone puts on a good front.

Richard's father, who died when Richard was nine, loved to take him to baseball games. Richard loved these occasions so much that he was able to describe in detail the games, where they sat in the stands, the scores of the various games, controversial plays, and other interesting sidelights. As he did so, he also was able to experience and share the intense sadness that had not previously been expressed verbally, although it had been inferred from his dramatic social withdrawal and significant drop in school grades in the six months following his father's death in a car accident. Eventually, as a result of his ability

69

to verbalize and share more of his grief, he became less withdrawn and his grades returned to their previous level.

Erik Erikson describes the ages six to twelve as the period when the child struggles with the issue of industry versus inferiority.[1] The sense of industry derives from feeling useful, a sense of being able to produce things and do them well. According to Erikson, the danger at this stage of development is a sense of inadequacy and/or inferiority. These middle years of childhood are a time of moving out from the protective womb of the family into a larger world of peers and adults outside the family. It is a time of developing important skills and competencies that determine one's standing among same-age cohorts and failure to do so results in feelings of inadequacy and low self-esteem.

These middle years of childhood are marked by rapid cognitive development. During this period children reach what Piaget called the stage of concrete operations. They become capable of far more sophisticated thought and mental operations than was possible during the preschool years. There is a reduction in the egocentrism of thought so characteristic of the preschool child. They become as Piaget states "decentered." No longer does the universe revolve around them. They become capable of looking at things from the other person's perspective and to see more than one dimension or aspect. Still they lack the capacity for abstract thinking that develops in adolescence.[2]

The ability to accomplish the tasks of the middle years depends upon having a secure base at home to which school-age children can return and receive support. If anything happens to undermine that secure base it can be expected that children will have more difficulty applying themselves to the age-appropriate tasks of developing their competencies and friendships. If the death of a parent or a sibling occurs during this developmental phase, it may lead to a serious setback in the efforts of children to attain a stronger sense of autonomy and competence in the larger world apart from family. If the death is preceded by a period of lengthy illness, the resources of the family may have been consumed in taking care of the sick family member and, thus, leaving little time, energy, and attention for the school-age child. Under such circumstances, the child's secure base is greatly undermined.

School-age children under nine years of age tend to have scary notions of death. Death is externalized in the form of ghosts or skeletons for this younger group. Beginning around age nine, school-age children perceive death as a natural and inevitable event. Even at this age, however, children may still view death as reversible. Helpers will need to explore with school-age children where they fall in this developmental progression of the understanding of death so that they can gear their interventions accordingly.

Helping the School-Age Child Grieve the Death of a Sibling

Children in this age group who have lost a sibling tend to manifest a wide gamut of feelings and behavior. In addition to their intense sadness, they frequently are quite angry that so much time and attention has been devoted to their seriously ill sibling. These resentments, often unexpressed verbally, leave children with a heavy burden of guilt at the time of death of their brother or sister. Fear of their own death is also commonly experienced by school-age children when a sibling dies.

Look for opportunities to intervene in a preventative way when children this age have a terminally ill sibling. You should normalize and universalize the feelings of hostility toward their seriously ill sibling. Since children this age have a very difficult time putting such sensitive feelings into words, a monologue might help them to get started. You might say, "I've talked with other boys and girls your age who have faced the same situation you're in. They had a brother or sister who was very ill. Often they have told me how very angry they sometimes feel that their sick brother or sister takes up so much of their parents' time, energy, and attention. They have told me how they feel there is little left over for them." It is good to relate this in a slow and deliberate manner with frequent pauses so that children have many opportunities to jump in and describe their experiences. The purpose of the monologue is to stimulate children to share their own feelings. If they are simply not ready to do this, at least they can benefit from knowing how other children feel so they need not feel so alone with their feelings. Sometimes children this age are genuinely surprised that others have similar feelings. In such a case, the monologues can have the effect of reducing the terrible sense of isolation, much of which is self-imposed because they assume that no one could possibly understand how they feel.

If children do not offer feelings of their own, it may be helpful to inquire, "What things make you angry about having a brother who has been so sick for so long?" If children do not respond but remain attentive, the monologue can continue: "Other children have told me that even though they get very mad about the situation, they also feel very sad and underneath their mad feelings are feelings of love for their sick brother or sister. Often they tell me it helps them to feel better if they make something for their brother or sister. It helps to remind them that they really do love their brother or sister." The purpose of this latter monologue is to affirm the love of children for the ill sibling, in spite of their angry feelings. Of course, this will be helpful to the ill sibling but also to the children in easing the burden of guilt when the sibling dies. Again, if children don't volunteer feelings, you might say, "No one knows better than you what would please your sister. What do you think you could make for her that will help you both remember that you really do love her?"

The monologue that hopefully becomes more of a dialogue as it proceeds can continue: "Children also tell me about how angry they feel toward their mom and dad. They sometimes tell me that they feel deserted because they have been so wrapped up in taking care of their brother or sister. Sometimes they have shared with me how badly they feel because they have these angry feelings toward their parents. They start to wonder if they are really bad for having such feelings. But I tell them over and over that they are not bad at all. Everyone gets angry. Kids and grown-ups get angry every day. And just because you get angry at someone it doesn't mean you don't love them anymore. We can love someone and be angry with them at the same time. (This is a concept that developmentally is difficult to grasp for the younger school-age child.) When you have feelings like that what helps you to feel better?"

Notice the question begins not with *if* but with *when*. Children respond better if feelings are normalized and it is only a question of what specific form they take for that particular child. It is also better to ask open-ended questions rather than closed questions that can be answered simply with a yes or no. Finally, this question seeks to elicit information about ways children cope with their most painful feelings.

Use simple and direct language in explaining death to a school-age child. It is helpful to explain death "as when the body totally stops working."[3] Since the school-age child thinks in concrete terms it may be helpful to remind him of his experience with the death of a pet. As with the pre-school child it is important to explain that most people live a long time but sometimes people get so badly hurt in accidents that the doctors and hospitals working as hard as they can still can't keep the body working.

Children in the five- to seven-year age group have some frightening notions of death. Death in this age group is often viewed as a spirit that comes for you. Young school-age children tend to view death as happening to those who can't run fast enough to get away from the spirit, such as the elderly, the handicapped, and the clumsy. These concepts in part reflect their need to deny that death could happen to them, which is one reason why the death of a sibling can be such a frightening experience.

Upon the death of a sibling, focus the school-age child on ways that he can feel less overwhelmed by his intense painful feelings. Children this age find it hard to tolerate painful feelings for any length of time. Martha Wolfenstein, a well-known psychoanalyst, referred to their "short sadness span." She and many other child development experts believe that a child's capacities for tolerating and bearing the powerful emotions of grief are quite limited.[4] There is controversy on this point, however, as mentioned in the first chapter. John Bowlby and Erna Furman are two highly regarded experts who have described rather extensive grief work undertaken with young, even preschool children.

Clearly, there are tremendous individual differences in the ability to grieve that have to be taken into account. Most authorities on this topic would support the notion that children in this age group would benefit from efforts to strengthen their coping and adaptive resources. This can be done by redirecting the focus, as described in detail by William Van Ornum and John Mordock in their book, *Crisis Counseling with Children and Adolescents,* from what makes the child anxious, sad, frightened, or angry to an examination of what makes him less anxious, sad, frightened, or angry.[5] This line of inquiry brings into view the existing resources of the child, including both inner resources as well as those that exist within his environment on which he can draw to cope with feelings and experiences that might otherwise be overwhelming.

Be sensitive to the compounding of difficulties for the bereaved school-age child. The anger these children feel toward their parents for neglecting them during this difficult time of crisis in the family is often compounded by the frequent marital difficulties that develop as a result of the severe strain on the relationship resulting from the loss of a child. Should the parents decide to separate and/or divorce, the child's guilt is multiplied many times since he may feel that his anger and difficult behavior may have been a prime contributing factor in the breakup of the marriage. With all of this going on at home, it is very difficult for such children to concentrate and be productive in the school setting. These compounded stresses are evident in the following vignette concerning Julie.

Julie was eight when her only sibling, Margaret, died at age ten after a long battle with leukemia. Julie was very sad in the months following her sister's death but also quite angry with her parents for being so preoccupied in the past with her sister's illness and now her death. She had also felt resentful toward her sister, which left her with considerable guilt. She especially suffered in guilty silence for having harbored death wishes toward Margaret during times when she felt especially ignored by the family. Julie also missed Margaret intensely as they had spent many hours playing together. Julie's bereavement was made all the more painful by the increasing fights between her parents. Julie was brought to counseling as a result of escalating negativistic and defiant behavior a month after her parents separated. In addition to the previous burden of guilt she now believed her trying behavior was instrumental in the father's decision to move out of the home.

Focus on building and reinforcing social skills. Children grieving for a lost sibling often cannot reach out to peers for companionship, which intensifies their pain and loneliness. They often lack the social skills and inner strength to seek out and connect with others. As they become increasingly angry and hurt about their unmet needs, they interact less with peers and significant others. The increasing withdrawal and cynicism of the children further cut them off from needed social support and positive reinforcement. This detrimental cycle can be interrupted by teaching age-appropriate social skills. Role-playing techniques can be used to coach children in developing skills such as initiating conversations and sharing feelings.

Counselors in schools should develop plans of action to deal with death and dying. Sandra Fox at the Judge Baker Guidance Center has developed the Good Grief Program, which includes excellent resource materials on death and dying for schools (see appendix for address). All schools should have a training program for teachers to assist them in dealing with the issue of death and dying. In the case of the death of a teacher or classmate a large number of children will be directly impacted. In the case of the death of a parent or sibling or friend of a child in the class the impact will be mostly on that one child but other youngsters may experience enormous fear and anxiety about their own vulnerability to such losses. Teachers need to be comfortable not only in offering support to an individual child but also in leading discussions and answering questions from the whole class on death and dying. If your school does not have a plan of action for dealing with death or a training program for teachers I urge you to start planning now. The worst time to do it is when you are faced with a crisis.

Helping School-Age Children Grieve the Death of a Parent

Children in the middle years who have lost a parent through death face very serious challenges in maintaining their developmental stride. The loss of a parent at a time when children are trying to develop mastery and competence in the extrafamilial world is a devastating blow. Not only do school-age children lose the support and caring of one of their parents but the remaining parent is often preoccupied with grief. In addition, the loss can have a destabilizing effect on the family equilibrium. Such was the case in Susan's family.

Susan was eight when her father who was a banker died after a brief illness. Susan was very close to her father and took his death very hard. Her grieving was doubly painful since she perceived her seven-year-old brother as her mother's favorite. She now felt rather isolated and alienated in the remaining family constellation. The rivalries between her and her brother intensified and caused such strain in the family that her grief-stricken mother felt overwhelmed. Thus, Susan reacted with bitterness to the loss not only of her father but also of an important alliance. In the remaining family, she felt a lack of acceptance from her mother. The preferred child, in this family the younger brother, also suffers. In addition to the exceedingly painful loss of a parent, such children often experience considerable guilt about their favored status in the remaining family composition. They also bear the brunt of the hostility and resentment of the nonpreferred sibling(s). In the face of these intense rivalries the surviving parents may feel overwhelmed with the task of parenting alone and may respond by abdicating their leadership role in the family. The surviving parents in these families as well as the children will need considerable support in order to prevent such dysfunctional patterns from developing.

Middle-years children understand more about death than preschool children. By the time children reach nine, many experts believe their conceptualization of death approximates that of an adult. Death is viewed as a natural process and many children realize it is irreversible. By this age children are also able to verbalize more of their feelings. Missy, aged nine, whose mother died, verbalized her fears, "I worry about my father every time he gets sick. My mom got sick in the summer and died before school started again." Children this age who lose one parent feel very vulnerable. One of their greatest fears is that they will lose the other parent too. Mitchell, seven at the time his father died, stated that "I am really afraid that something will happen to Mom while she sleeps. I am also afraid of robbers coming in at night. I never was afraid when my father was here." Peter, whose mother died of cancer when he was eleven, confided, "I am always worried that something could happen to my dad, like cancer. I guess, I'd have to go to boarding school. I even worry when he gets a cold, because that's how it started with my mother."

Encourage verbalization of conflictual feelings. Due to their increasing verbal skills school-age children can sometimes express the conflictual and ambivalent feelings that, when unexpressed, can block the grieving process. Jerry, aged ten, confided in counseling that he is angry with his mother that she can't be like his deceased father. In death, it is typical for children to idealize the lost parent and displace their anger and frustration onto the remaining parent. Jenny, aged nine, worried that since she cries less about the death of her father than her younger sister that her mother and sister will feel that she didn't love her father as much. Verbalizing feelings such as these enables school-age children to organize their inner experiences. The act of framing into words one's feelings and perceptions leads to better integration of one's internal world. The active sharing of these feelings and perceptions with a trusted person can lessen the pain of bereavement.

Many children this age find it hard to acknowledge their anger toward the deceased parent. The anger may relate to the sense of desertion and abandonment they feel in relation to the death itself or it might relate to disappointments in the relationship. Willie, age seven, reluctantly after much encouragement, finally admitted he was angry with his father for drinking so much, which he felt (with justification) had contributed to his father's early death. Although Willie had previously idealized his deceased father while angrily lashing out at his mother and refusing to do his work at school, he now gradually began to share his anger about an earlier felt desertion. He and his father had been very close during the early years and had gone many places together. When his father started drinking heavily these shared activities occurred less and less. This unexpressed resentment toward his father for which he felt very guilty was blocking the forward progress of Willie's grief work. As he was slowly able to evolve a more realistic picture of his father and achieve a balance between his positive and negative feelings, he was able to let go of his emotional investment in his deceased father. As a consequence his relationship with his mother and his work in school began to improve. He also became more interested in socializing with his peers from whom he had become isolated after the death of his father.

Monologues may be useful in eliciting these sensitive feelings in some children at this age. You might say, "In talking with other boys and girls your age whose parent has died, they have told me some interesting things about their feelings. While they have often talked to me about how much they loved their mom or dad who died, they also have told me about feeling quite angry with their mom or dad. Sometimes, they feel angry just because their mom or dad died. One boy said, "How dare he die right now. He promised to help me learn how to hit the ball better and to come watch all my games in Little League." Parents aren't supposed to die when kids are young. They tell me how angry they feel that their friends have both parents and they only have one. Sometimes they tell me about specific times when their parent got angry with them for what they felt was not a good reason. A girl told me, "My mom was so cranky in the weeks before she died. She was always yelling and sometimes she would get mad at me for things my brother was doing. It really made me so mad." When boys and girls tell me about these angry feelings they seem to feel better because then they can more easily remember the good times with their mom and dad and are able to hold on to those warm, happy memories."

In the above monologue, not only are the ambivalent feelings articulated and normalized, but explicit encouragement is offered for the expression of such feelings. You should take a clear position and state that it is good to express these feelings because children are often fearful that putting such feelings into words is an act of betrayal toward the dead parent and will lead to punishment. Finally, their guilt is lessened when they are assured that after expressing the negative feelings they will more easily be able to remember the happy times and feel the loving feelings toward their deceased parent. *This balancing of feelings is something that you need to help children with lest they feel too exposed when they express the negative side of their ambivalent feelings.*

Encourage school-age children to put their sadness into words. A noted analyst, Helene Deutsch, in a paper entitled "The Absence of Grief," focused on the indifference that children so frequently manifest following the death of a loved one.[6] Robert, age eight, learned that the telephone call to his mother was the hospital informing her that his father had died. Robert cried hard for a few minutes and then went out and played ball with his friends. It is important not to misinterpret this developmentally normal response as "heartless" or uncaring behavior.[7] The capacities of the school-age child are not sufficiently developed to bear the strain of the work of mourning in the prolonged and intense way typical of adult grieving. Nevertheless, children of this age do feel deep sadness and longing and need to be encouraged to put these feelings into words. They may not be able to stay with these feelings for very long and, once having shared them, may feel a need to retreat and talk about other things. However, in stages, they can accomplish a significant amount of grief work. They need to distract and distance themselves from the sadness at times and they need to experience it and express it directly at other times. These needs are reflected in the responses of an eight-year-old girl whose father had died to the question of what had helped the most in coping with her grief. Her reply was: "Number 1, keep your mind off being sad. Number 2, get up in the morning, even if you don't feel like it. Number 3, let out your sadness." In response to the same question a seven-year-old boy said: "Go ahead and cry and cry." When the same boy was asked this question at a different time he replied, "Don't deal with it, set feelings aside. Don't always think about it." It is important to sense when children need to distract themselves and think about other things or just be left alone and when they need to put their sadness into words and share their feelings with a trusted adult.

Encourage the verbal expression of feelings by reviewing memories of the lost parent. You should pursue detailed descriptions of favorite memories. The more detailed and vivid the recollection, the more likely children will be able to experience the feelings of sadness, missing, and longing that need to be acknowledged and shared. If children say that they liked to go fishing with their deceased dad, you can ask about a specific time when they went fishing or a time when something funny happened such as getting their fishing lines tangled up or someone fell into the stream.

Some experts believe that successful resolution of mourning is directly proportional to the ability of children to acknowledge, tolerate, and express their feelings of intense sadness and longing. This is a capacity that is developmentally influenced. The older the child, the greater is the capacity. But even the quite young child is capable of expressing intense sadness at least for brief periods. It is therefore quite important for you to create as many opportunities as possible for children to put their sadness into words. Jerry with encouragement in counseling was able to express his intense pain:

Jerry was seven when his father died of a sudden and massive heart attack. Jerry's father used to take him on weekends to the firehouse where his father was a volunteer. Jerry would help his dad and other volunteer firemen wash the truck and sometimes ride in it with his father to get gas. When such memories were pursued in counseling, Jerry inevitably would feel his sadness and longing and this would be expressed both in words and in tears, and sometimes in heartrending sobs.

Utilize symbolic and dramatic play and drawings for those children unable to verbalize. Preschool children are more likely to work out their feelings through drawings and play, while school-age children rely more on verbalization to organize and make sense of their experiences.[8] Younger children in this age group, however, may still find that puppet, dollhouse, and dramatic play provide them with the psychological distance they need to work out their feelings. By playing out scenes in which Freddy the Frog is teased by Harry the Skunk and Billy the Turtle because he doesn't have a father, children learn gradually to master some of the feelings that they would find overpowering if they were to approach them more directly.

Sometimes the degree of rage and underlying powerlessness and helplessness expressed through the symbolic play is striking in these children who have suffered such major losses.[9] With each repetition of the play they gradually acquire more of a sense of mastery that allows them eventually to integrate the experiences.

Counselors should take a nondirective approach in working therapeutically with the play of bereaved children. They are relying on symbolic play as a mode of expression because they lack sufficient psychological resources to deal with the pain more directly. To confront or interpret the underlying meaning of the play of these children is to "blow their cover." This is likely to be experienced as intrusive and insensitive by children who trusted the counselor to understand that they needed the safety of the symbolic play characters to work on resolving their feelings.

Children who use symbolic play in this way to gain some safe distance from potentially overwhelming feelings of-

ten do reach a point where they can directly talk about
their feelings. I recommend, however, that you follow
their lead so that the children are giving clear and specific
indications that they are ready to talk about their feelings
directly. I have had children in the midst of symbolic play
turn to me and say, "You know something like that happened to me once." In such a case you can pursue with
the child his/her feelings directly.

Children age seven and over typically do not engage
in symbolic play or dramatic enactments. Children in this
age group are usually more interested in sports, board
games, and rule-governed games of all kinds. The interest
in rules and conventions at this age is considered to be
a way children internalize the rules and regulations of
authority so that they are less dependent on the presence
of adults.[10] Children, however, who have suffered major
losses in their early life may be functioning developmentally, particularly emotionally, at much younger levels than
indicated by their chronological age. Many of these children will find the use of puppets and various dramatic
enactments appealing in an effort to resolve their feelings.

I have many times found myself playing a spirited game
of hide-and-seek with school-age children who have lost
a parent. This game along with its more infantile version
of peek-a-boo is played the world over by children trying
to master the feelings of fear regarding separation and
loss. The high drama and tension experienced by the child
when in the process of hiding and seeking attests to the
psychological importance of the mastery being sought.

In addition to symbolic and dramatic play, one very important mode of expression for children in the middle
years of childhood is artwork and drawings. When doing
nondirected drawing or painting some children are able
to give expression to feelings in a symbolic way that they
would be blocked in expressing verbally. I have found

structured drawing activities to be particularly useful with the school-age bereaved children. I often ask children to draw a picture of their deceased parent and them doing something together. Then I will direct them to add gradually to the collection pictures of special and favorite things they did together, family trips and vacations, holidays, birthday parties, and funny things that happened along the way.

Once it is down on paper it is easier to get children to talk about the details of the experience, which often brings into focus the feelings that have been so hard for them to express. If, for example, one of their favorite memories is a family trip to Disneyland, once they draw a picture of it, it becomes more concrete and real. It is then much easier to engage them in a give-and-take discussion about all the things that happened that made it such a special time for them and to explore the associated feelings. In this way creative expression through artistic productions should be encouraged by helpers who find children this age verbally reticient and inhibited.

Other children who may be relatively nonverbal may express themselves freely through poems or songs that they write. Still other verbally inhibited children may be able to express themselves much more freely through writing in diaries or journals that they can be encouraged to keep and to share if they are not too private. I have found with children that if their privacy is respected and you make it clear that they are entitled to keep their feelings and thoughts to themselves they usually end up wanting to share them with you. Of course, it should be emphasized here that none of these strategies should be undertaken as a ploy. If it is done in a manipulative way, children will quickly see through the insincerity and will start to mistrust you.

In a similar approach, I have sometimes asked children

to bring favorite photographs to the counseling session that then serve as springboards for sharing of memories and feelings. I have also asked school-age bereaved children to draw pictures of objects and favorite possessions that link them to their lost parent.[11] Sometimes this is something that was given to them by the deceased parent. Often, it was a cherished possession of the deceased parent that everyone in the family associates with the lost parent, such as a particular coffee mug, favorite chair, or old hat. You can also ask children to bring these "linking objects" to the sessions; they can be emotionally impactful and especially useful for those youngsters manifesting what appears to be the "absence of grief" as described by Deutsch.[12] Obviously, children should not be pressured into doing this if they show signs of not being ready to confront their feelings. Such signs might include obvious anxiety when the request is made to bring in such objects or an inability or unwillingness to draw them. Forgetting to bring them in after agreeing to do so may also suggest they are not ready. In this case the counselor can indicate that "we will wait until a time that is more comfortable for you."

Discuss the funeral with school-age children to assist the grieving process. Most authorities would agree that children in this age group should be permitted and even encouraged to attend the funeral. Children should not be forced to go if they strongly resist but most children will choose to go and participate in the rituals of mourning that are valued by their family. Children not permitted to participate may feel left out of a very important family occasion and resent it as was the case with Jimmy.

Jimmy was eight when his father died. The family thought it best for him to stay with an aunt on the day of the funeral. Six months later in counseling he expressed considerable rage that he had been denied the opportunity to be a part of the family's observance of his father's death. I was very much surprised ten years later when Jimmy as a college student reentered counseling because he was facing some relationship difficulties that he was still quite resentful about his exclusion from his father's funeral.

In helping children this age to grieve, it can be beneficial to ask them about the funeral. Ask them what they liked and didn't like about it. Inquire about what was said regarding their deceased parent. The burial and visits to the cemetery can also be pursued in terms of feelings. Children who have not gone to the cemetery can be encouraged to go. Ask children if they have conversations with the dead parent at the cemetery or at other times. Find out what they take to put on the grave and who goes with them. Ask what the headstone looks like and what is written on it. All of these questions make the death more real and may be especially useful for those children who display "absence of grief" or "short sadness span."

Avoid falling in the trap of not recognizing that the children who need encouragement to grieve the most often receive it the least. Children who show few outward signs of grief may receive little comfort or encouragement to mourn because of the strong need of the adults to deny the pain of grief in children. If children appear to be adjusting there will be a strong temptation to leave well enough alone. Unfortunately, this often leads to a truncated grieving process and makes it more likely that the grief will be expressed in either a delayed or distorted form.

Boys in this age group are likely to express distorted grief through aggressive behavior while girls tend to exhibit compulsive caregiving behavior.[13] The aggressive behavior of the boys and sometimes girls as well can be viewed as an angry protest that is similar to the "angry unwillingness" described in chapter 1. Compulsive care-

giving in girls may take the form of becoming "little mothers." They may assume the care of younger siblings in
an exaggerated fashion. This can be a way of denying
sadness and strong longings for the deceased parent and
dispensing the care that they themselves so sorely miss.
When parents and caregivers are sensitive to the needs
of these children and help them express their missing
and yearning for the lost parent they may be able to prevent these distorted patterns of grief from developing.

*Remember that the key to assisting children to grieve is by
forming a trusting relationship, wherein gradually children will
feel safe enough to share their feelings of longing and sadness.*
This will take time and your sincerity as a counselor/
helper will be tested and very likely retested. Since children have experienced on an emotional level the desertion
of someone they loved and depended on when their parent died, they naturally may expect that you will desert
them too. Children may press for a premature ending
to the helping relationship as a way of avoiding such an
eventuality. This defensive tactic follows the principle of
"You can't fire me, I quit!" Basically, children are expressing through their behavior the reluctance to trust so that
they never have to go through again the almost-unbear-
able pain of loss. This struggle was poignantly expressed
by Russell Baker in his autobiography *Growing Up*.[14] He
describes how he learned at age six that his father had
died and he stated, "After that I never cried again with
any real conviction, nor expected much of anyone's God
except indifference, nor loved deeply without fear that
it would cost me deeply in pain" (p. 81).

You will need to persist in your expressions of concern
and interest at those very points when children may wish
to break off the contact. You will need to be active and
quite explicit in your wish to stay with them as you journey
together along the winding and bumpy road that leads

to mastering grief. It is sometimes very helpful to anticipate with children resistance to continuing this work. You
might say, "There are going to be times when talking
about your sadness and missing your father is going to
hurt and you might not want to come back and talk anymore. If we keep working at it together though, there
will come a day when you can remember your father and
talk about him without the hurting you feel now."

Utilize the family system for maximum impact. Individual sessions with children may be indicated in those instances
where the surviving parent is too grief-stricken to assist
and encourage the child's mourning or where the child's
protective stance toward the parent would inhibit the
mourning process. In many cases meeting with the surviving family unit together will be most advantageous because it recognizes the reality of the remaining family
composition. Also, the mutual sharing of grief and the
offering of support to one another can build a sense of
cohesion and unity. By encouraging the open expression
of grief you give permission to all family members to
mourn, thus reducing the inhibiting influence of protective responses to each other. When children are seen sepa-
rately, it is vitally important to meet also with the surviving
parent to offer support and to guide the parent in assisting the children to grieve.

Many parents are unsure as to whether it is good for
them to show their own grief to their children and how
much to encourage children in expression of their sadness. Parents should be encouraged to share their own
feelings of grief as long as this is accompanied by the
reassurance "that we will make it through this and one
day it won't hurt so much." Once they understand that
it is healthy for children to express their sadness and longing to the fullest extent they can, many parents very sensitively and capably facilitate the grieving process in their

children. Often much more is accomplished by working through the parents than could ever be accomplished by working with the children alone. Because of highly ambivalent relationships with the deceased parent or excessive guilt that complicates the grieving process some children will need individual counseling sessions in addition to the encouragement and support they receive in their families.

Helping School-Age Children Grieve the Loss of Grandparents

Grandparents can play such a special role in the lives of young children that their loss can be exceedingly painful for children even though continuity of care is not usually threatened as it is with the death of a parent. The death of a grandparent is a much more frequent occurrence in the life of children than the death of a parent and the death of a grandparent for many children is their first personal experience with death. Just as in the case of the death of a parent, a grandparent's death can arouse considerable anxiety regarding the child's own mortality, in addition to representing a very significant personal loss. The death of a grandparent can also stir fears of the loss of parents. The degree of loss experienced by children will vary with the quality of the attachment to the grandparent and sometimes is quite profound. The following are comments from school-age children who had experienced the death of a grandparent:

"My grandfather was the greatest guy ever. I couldn't believe when he died. He was so strong. He had been in the army. I thought for sure he would survive his stroke. I was in shock."

"The first month after my grandmother died, I just

felt like I wanted to die myself. I missed her so much. I can't believe she is dead and will never come back. She made me feel so special. I loved going to her house."

"My grandfather was my special pal. He taught me how to fish and he even played baseball with me. He came to all of my games and I used to go to his house a lot. We talked about a lot of things and we would watch the football games on TV together. I don't know what to do. I keep thinking about him. I wish he was here. I feel so sad, especially on the weekends."

These children need encouragement and permission to grieve just as surely as the child who loses a parent. If they are supported in their grieving for the grandparent they will be far better equipped to face the inevitable deaths and losses that come as they proceed through the life cycle.

Referring School-Age Children for Psychotherapy

While the vast majority of bereaved school-age children will benefit from grief counseling, a small minority may require psychotherapy that can take many forms including individual or family therapy. As with all ages, sudden and unexpected deaths, and traumatic deaths (e.g., murder or suicide) are more likely to result in complicated bereavement. In addition, as with all ages, an excessively dependent or conflicted relationship with the deceased increases the risk of pathological mourning. Signs of post-traumatic stress disorder delineated in the previous chapter would indicate need for psychotherapy. Likewise if school-age children manifest post-traumatic play (see chapter 2) a referral should be made to a mental health professional who specializes in child therapy. The functioning of school-age bereaved children in the three critical areas of family, school, and social life should be carefully reviewed and monitored. As with younger children, regression is common and a wide range of stress-related reactions are normal including a temporary return to bed-wetting, sleep difficulties, various somatic symptoms, and a decline in school grades. The more areas where the child is having difficulty functioning, and the longer it continues, the more likely a referral for psychotherapy is warranted. The child-mental-health professional can make a determination as to whether individual or family therapy or in some cases group therapy is needed. In most cases, a successful outcome is enhanced by involving the family in the therapy as fully as possible.

Summary

School-age children have a difficult time tolerating for prolonged periods their feelings of intense sadness and loss as well as the other painful feelings of grief: fear, anger, and guilt. They can be helped to grieve, nevertheless, by sensitive and empathic helpers who can sense when they need to express their feelings and when they need to be left alone. Helpers can also assist them to develop the ego defenses and coping capacities that will enable them to bear the strain of the grief work so that there is less chance that the grief will be delayed or expressed in a distorted manner. A number of strategies and techniques to assist the school-age child in grieving were discussed with the primary aim of preventing grief from arresting or interfering with the developmental process.

4

Helping Adolescents to Grieve

Death of a Parent

In Judy Blume's book *Tiger Eyes* she describes how fifteen-year-old Davey is deeply absorbed in thought.[1] She vividly depicts how Davey focuses on her tight-fitting shoes borrowed from her mother, and the pain from the blisters forming on her toes so that she doesn't have to think about the coffin that she is standing in front of and that her father's body is inside.

Davey's father has been killed in a robbery in his store in Atlantic City and the loss completely shatters the assumptions and beliefs she has held about life up to that point. During the next two weeks she does not shower, spends most of the time in bed, and only leaves the house once for a short walk with her boyfriend. Because of the constant painful reminders of the tragedy Davey and her mother and younger brother soon move to New Mexico to live with her aunt and uncle. Her world will never be the same again.

Judy Blume's poignant story is all the more moving because of the timing of this teenager's loss of her father. Early adolescent girls benefit from affirmation by their fathers of their physical attractiveness as well as validation of their self-worth generally. The loss of their father during this period can be a devastating blow to their self-esteem.

Although adolescents have developed a solid concept of death, they typically are profoundly shaken by personal experiences with death. When death strikes within the family or among close friends the very core of their assumptive world is thrown into turmoil. Their sense of vulnerability is heightened because their ability to contemplate their own death is much greater than preschoolers and school-age children. At the very time when they are moving away from the family and becoming more and more invested in relationships with peers, the death of a parent can undermine their emerging sense of autonomy or lead to an exaggerated sense of self-sufficiency, a kind of pseudoindependence.

Adolescents need something firm to bounce off of, to separate from. As much as they might resent parents who nag them about homework, the hours they keep, or the speed that they drive, all of these represent needed boundaries and structure that form the backdrop for the adolescent quest for identity. When a parent dies the structure is shaken, especially if the remaining parent feels overwhelmed with the task of guiding one or more adolescents all alone.

Adolescent bereavement has to be viewed in the context of the importance that peer relationships assume during this developmental stage. Although it is important for healthy mourning that adolescents be able to express their intense yearning for the lost loved person, they will not do so if they feel that this sets them apart or makes them different from their peers. The overriding motivation for the typical teenager is to fit in. Due to their own uncomfortableness and lack of preparation in death-related matters peers may not know how to respond in a comforting and supportive way to a bereaved adolescent. One high school boy's friends were afraid to tell jokes in his presence or invite him to parties after his father died.[2] Fortunately, this is not always the case. Some adolescents who have prior experiences with bereavement can be very consoling and helpful to their peers at times of loss. Adolescents who can turn to understanding peers at the time of the death of a parent will feel less threatened by the powerful urges to be more childlike that a major loss evokes. Such urges are threatening to adolescents because their sense of independence is still so shaky.

Regardless of how supportive their peer group may be, teens will still need the support and understanding of their surviving family in order to master the grieving process. Adolescents, much more than school-age and preschool children, will be in conflict about the appropriate role they should play in the surviving family. Early adolescents have just begun the process of removing themselves from the family while later adolescents may be well removed and highly invested in extrafamilial relationships. The death of a parent can be expected to have different effects on these youths depending on where they are in the family-emancipation process. Terry and Michelle are examples of adolescents whose development was adversely impacted by the burdensome roles they felt compelled to take on in their families and by their inability to grieve for the lost parent because there was little support for doing so.

Terry was thirteen when his mother died after a long illness lasting four years. He had been close to his mother and experienced her death as a great loss. He perceived his father as uninterested in his activities including sports even though Terry was an excellent athlete. He was called on to assume much responsibility for his younger siblings. When Terry appeared for counseling ten years later, the loss of his mother was still very much unresolved and he complained bitterly of missing out on a playful, care-free childhood. Having been overburdened early in life by the care of his terminally ill mother and his younger siblings, in young adult life he felt "trapped" by the responsibilities of his business and his marriage. Many of his adjustment difficulties to adult life could be traced to the lack of encouragement and support for mourning the loss of his mother as an early adolescent.

Michelle was fifteen when her father died of a massive heart attack. Because her mother was chronically depressed following her father's death, she felt the need to assume her father's role in the family and allow her dependent mother to lean on her. As a result Michelle, although a strikingly pretty girl, developed very little social life during her teen years and did not date any boys. In many ways her adolescent development came to an abrupt halt with the death of her father. When she entered counseling during her college years she still felt a very heavy responsibility for her mother and had not really begun grieving for her father.

Do nothing to interfere with the natural outpouring of acute pain, sadness, anger, and guilt in the immediate aftermath of the loss. Upon first learning of death, some adolescents may be able to give expression to their acute grief by crying and crying. This is a time to simply sit with adolescents in their grief. Being an attentive listener and a sympathetic visible presence and nothing else may be very difficult for caregivers.[3] The temptation is to do more. Helpers would like to relieve the intense suffering but this can interfere with the natural healing process of grievers learning to express and tolerate their painful feelings. We have to learn to tolerate our own sense of helplessness since there really is nothing we can do to spare grievers their pain. We can, however, reframe the way we view what is real help in this situation. In the instance of acute grief, real help is being an interested companion who sits with the bereaved until they can bear their pain more easily.

Teens also need to be given permission not to grieve. School-age children can be overwhelmed at times with their painful feelings of bereavement and need permission to distract themselves temporarily from the grief. This applies to teens as well. *After* adolescents have cried and cried and talked and talked about the loss with friends, with family, and with helpers, a point may be reached where any further focus on the loss at that moment would not be useful. A suggestion that teenagers might enjoy getting out for a while with their friends to see a movie may be appropriate. This gives them permission not to grieve all the time and suggests that it is not an act of disloyalty to the deceased parent to enjoy life again and that there is a future without the deceased parent.

Encourage adolescents to express their longing, yearning, and sadness. Adolescents like Terry and Michelle need direct and explicit encouragement to grieve since the wish to avoid and escape these painful feelings is so typical of adolescents.[4] There will always be distractions, the powerful tendency to deny the loss, roles to be assumed, jobs to be done, and friends to join in various diversionary pursuits. Teens need to talk about their feelings and their memories with a trusted, objective person who can really listen in an empathic way. This will help to prevent the unhealthy and aborted grief process that so adversely impacted the adolescent development of Michelle and Terry.

Help adolescents understand the normal grieving process. Since adolescents fear regression and loss of emotional control, it is important to assure them that the wide-ranging responses of acute grief are normal including the feeling that "I am losing my mind." It is also critical to assure them that these manifestations of acute grief will pass. They need to know they will survive the pain and that they will be able someday to remember the deceased parent without the distress they feel now. They should know that irritability, inability to sleep, loss of appetite, preoccupation with the deceased, anxiety, anger, and guilt are all common reactions during acute grief.

Stress the unique form grief will take for each person. Like younger children, teens may compare their reactions to other family members. If their own grief, at least outwardly, is less intense they may feel that this appears to others that they loved the parent less. This results in an unnecessary burden of guilt. As mentioned in chapter 3, these differences may in fact lead to misunderstandings within the family and accusations such as, "You didn't love your dad very much if you can't even cry!" So you need to help not only the adolescent but also the entire family to understand the wide range of ways to express grief.

Assist teens in grappling with some of the abstract mysteries of death. Adolescents are capable of formal operational thought; this means that they are capable of dealing with abstractions that would be beyond the grasp of younger children. This newly achieved capacity may lead to numerous questions about the philosophical and religious teachings on death and to a struggle to understand the meaning of life and death. You need to explore these questions patiently in an honest and open exchange with adolescents. You should simply acknowledge that you don't know in response to the questions that are unanswerable. If you are not sure what you believe with respect to a religious teaching or a philosophical view regarding death, this should be stated honestly—e.g., "I am not sure what I believe about that, but some people believe (or some religions teach). . . ."

Address the anxiety that personal death awareness evokes in adolescents. The shield of invulnerability is shattered by the death of a parent. The death of a family member or perhaps even more of a peer can't help but focus adolescents on their own mortality. Since our society so strongly colludes in denial of death, this may be one of those rare occasions when the adolescent is forced to contemplate his own finite and fragile existence. Such an experience can evoke considerable anxiety. You need to enable bereaved adolescents to put into some reasonable perspective their own remote chances of dying any time soon. It is typical for youngsters to fear dying of the same illness or suffering the same accidental fate that has befallen their parent or peer.

Help the family to respect the need of bereaved adolescents for solitude. In my discussions with adolescents about what has been most beneficial to them in coping with their grief, the need for occasional solitude has been mentioned frequently. Adolescents need privacy and this should be recognized by parents and helpers. In times of major stress, adolescents particularly find it helpful to have some time alone. Unless this need takes the form of extreme withdrawal it should be supported by the family and helpers. The ideal situation is a balance between talking and sharing feelings with friends and trusted adults and some time alone to regroup and reflect on all that has happened.

Be sensitive to the sex roles difference in adolescent bereavement. Experts on adolescent bereavement have suggested a differential response to death by teenage boys and girls.[5] Male adolescents often behave more aggressively, frequently challenging authority and increasing their use of alcohol and drugs. These actions are a way of punishing others and themselves, relieving anxiety, and calling attention to their plight. Teenage girls, by contrast, often express a longing for comfort and reassurance along with an intense need to be held and consoled. These differential responses are illustrated by Peter, age sixteen, and Cary, age seventeen, when they entered counseling. Peter had lost his father nine months before as a result of cancer. Up until his father's terminal illness, Peter had been an excellent student and athlete with plans to attend college and go into engineering. Peter had been abusing pot and alcohol in the two months prior to counseling. The night before the first session, he had gone out drinking with his friends and showed up drunk after curfew at the home of one of his friends. He created such a scene that his friend's mother called the police. Peter was willing to talk and gradually began really to grieve for his father for the first time. Over a period of six months he shared many emotionally significant memories of his father and expressed much anger and sadness. Consequently, his acting out behavior largely subsided.

Cary's father had died of a cerebral aneurism eighteen months prior to the start of counseling. Cary had adored her father but, tragically, on that day they had an argument and weren't speaking to each other when he fell to the floor dead. Cary had not gone to the cemetery since the funeral and found it extremely difficult to discuss the loss. She had gone through a series of boyfriends. Each one had been idealized to the point that he got frightened by the intensity of her feelings and he would break off the relationship. This self-defeating pattern of seeking the lost relationship with her father through idealized relationships with older boyfriends yielded only after she was able to talk about her intense guilt and anger concerning her father's death. After that she was able to go to the grave and openly and deeply grieve for him.

Be sensitive to the increased guilt associated with the deidealization process in early adolescence. During early adolescence normal development entails a disillusioning process whereby originally idealized parents become deidealized.[6]

The previously admired parents become the object of criticism and severe faultfinding. In most adolescents this reappraisal of parents serves to increase autonomy and strengthen sense of self. In some adolescents, however, the inability to maintain the idealized images of the parents may result in a sense of loss and even depression. If a parent dies during early adolescence the guilt may be especially severe, given the sharp and often greatly exaggerated criticisms directed toward the parents during this stage. You can universalize this parental disillusionment process so that adolescents don't suffer undue guilt for having been so harsh in their judgments toward their deceased parent. The bereavement may be further complicated because the parents find this period very hard to tolerate themselves. Harsh words may be exchanged from both sides leaving much residual anger to be resolved. This residual resentment may inhibit grieving in the adolescent. The adolescent needs to be encouraged to express these resentments and to be helped to gain perspective on the whole disillusioning process.

Respond empathically to the vulnerable sense of self of adolescents. Anna Freud observed what she termed the normalcy of adolescent turmoil.[7] Adolescents are frequently noted to be subject to wide swings of mood. They lack a firm sense of identity. Their self-esteem tends to fluctuate wildly. Grandiose fantasy and behavior are intended to compensate for the underlying shaky self-concept. In short, adolescents manifest in varying degrees a vulnerable sense of self.[8] Given this developmental vulnerability, the death of a parent poses a major challenge to the psychological equilibrium of adolescents. You, therefore, should utilize ego-strengthening and ego-supportive interventions. Such interventions would include identifying and supporting healthy coping patterns (such as distraction when the pain is too great), discouraging unhealthy coping responses (such as alcohol or drug abuse or antisocial behavior) and facilitating the search for more adaptive alternatives. Interventions would also include education about the normal grief process. Adolescents should be encouraged to express their feelings and these feelings should then be validated. Difficult moments that lie ahead should be anticipated and plans developed to help cope with them. The love of teens for their deceased parent should be affirmed and their strength and positive resources highlighted. You should also keep in perspective that although turmoil is the normal lot for teenagers, it is often short-lived and manageable. Studies have indicated, in fact, that the majority of adolescents do not exhibit significant behavioral or emotional disturbance in spite of the stresses and rapid physiological, psychological, and social changes of this phase of life.[9]

Support the developmentally critical process of individuation in bereaved adolescents. Adolescence has been referred to as the "second individuation phase" of development.[10] This follows the separation-individuation phase of early childhood when the child makes his first attempts to reduce dependence on the mother in order to explore the environment.[11] The longing for autonomy is intense in the teenager and may lead to an exaggerated display of self-determination in ways that are disruptive to the family. This sometimes takes the form of extreme rebellion or even delinquency. The drive toward greater autonomy strengthens with adolescent maturation and is not completed until late adolescence or early adulthood.[12] If the death of a parent occurs in late adolescence there may be sufficient developmental force and momentum to enable the separation-individuation process to go forward. If the death occurs in early adolescence as it did in the lives of Michelle and Terry, the accomplishment of this developmental step may be seriously impeded. You need

to offer encouragement and support to the healthy auton-
omous drives in the youngster and also to support the
remaining parent to foster this growth process in the teenager. In the cases of Michelle and Terry the surviving
parent's lack of encouragement for their children's growing independence was a significant factor in the overbur-
dening of these two youngsters with adult responsibilities.
These parents themselves lacked the support they needed
to deal with their own grief and heavy responsibilities;
thus, they turned to their adolescent son and daughter
to relieve their overwhelming burdens. You can assist a
family to pursue alternatives or a division of responsibility
so that no one is impeded in growth and development.

*Recognize the critical importance that same sex friendships
have for early adolescents in terms of identity formation.* No
longer a child, the adolescent needs to find a new identity.
Same sex friendships play a crucial role in the search for
this new identity.[13] Bereaved teens are likely to turn to
their peers for comfort and solace. Yet teens will also need
the support of their family and other trusted adults as
well. Frequently, when bereaved adolescents are seen in
counseling they are quick to inform the counselor that
they have their friends to turn to and they don't have
that much to talk about with the adult. You should explic-
itly state that it is good that they have such meaningful
friendships and that they are confiding in their friends.
Often with a small amount of encouragement teenagers
will begin to share with adults as well. It is crucial to show
adolescents that you are sensitive to and recognize the
importance of friends in their lives.

*Be alert to the fantasized ideal family as another source of
guilt.* Teens not only seek a new identity for themselves
through the mirror of their peer friendships but also
search for ideal adults.[14] It is frequently observed that the
parents of friends are considered superior and may even

represent a fantasized ideal family. These idealized parent substitutes aid the adolescent search for identity by offering a greater diversity of models. They also assist the process of separation from the close dependent relationship with the parents. This very healthy and normal developmental search for substitute parents and families, however, can greatly intensify the guilt of adolescents whose parent dies during this stage. You need to assist adolescents in normalizing the feelings and behavior of this identity quest.

Recognize the many forms of adolescent rebellion and its implications for bereaved adolescents. Rebellion serves to put distance between adolescents struggling for independence and their parents. Outright forms of rebellion are easily recognized and consist of defiance, angry outbursts, and challenges of all kinds to adult authority. Some adolescents, however, may be outwardly conforming while engaging in fantasies of hostile and destructive attacks on teachers and parents.[15] Others may alternate between defiant and conforming behavior. Still others express their rebellion through sullen or angry moods while maintaining compliance with basic rules and expectations.[16] All forms of rebellion can intensify the guilt of bereaved adolescents whose parent has died. In addition, while the rebellion may be in the service of accomplishing an important developmental task, it nevertheless leads to much strain between the parents and adolescent. In the heat of battle hurtful words get exchanged and both sides often regret what they have said. Mike, a fifteen-year-old, was engaged in a bitter power struggle with his father who didn't like his hair style or length. In the midst of their emotionally charged interchange, Mike shouted, "I wish you would have a heart attack and die!" Fortunately, Mike's father is still alive and after a few days Mike cooled off enough to go back to his father and apologize for his remarks. Such futile power struggles are common in the lives of families with adolescents. If a parent in such a family dies, bereavement is complicated by the guilt stemming from such bitter exchanges and also by residual hurt and anger. Such feelings lead to a high degree of ambivalence that can inhibit the grief process. You will need to encourage the adolescent to verbalize both sides of the ambivalence so that the conflict (which some adolescents describe more like a war that is being waged inside) can be externalized and thereby lessened. Eventually a balance between the conflicting feelings can be achieved. This will be a challenging task, however, because the intense guilt associated with the negative side of the ambivalence will make the adolescent very reluctant to talk about these feelings.

Reach out to shy and inhibited teens to facilitate their grieving. Those youths who experience a painful verbal paralysis in social situations can be expected to have a particularly difficult time expressing their grief in words. Counselors working in school systems should develop plans of action for reaching out to reluctant grievers (see the Good Grief program listed in the appendix). Some of the techniques utilized with nonverbal school-age children may be useful with these teens such as monologues, drawings, and journal writing. Try to find the most natural mode of expression for a particular adolescent and encourage its use. Ask if they already keep a diary or a journal. You may be surprised to find out that many of these nonverbal youths have already developed other methods of self-expression. Another strategy useful with some reluctant grievers is to ask them to write a letter to the deceased parent and bring it to the counseling session. It is best to have them read the letter in the session. The healing effect derives from their sharing their feelings at a time when they are directly experiencing them with someone they have grown to trust. An alternative ritual that has been beneficial with some inhibited teens is to ask them to write a letter to the deceased parent and read it at the grave. It is usually recommended that they ask a trusted person to go with them so that they will be able to share the feelings that arise with a significant other.

Be prepared to tolerate anger and hostility in dealing with adolescents in acute grief. Anger toward the helpers who cannot make the pain go away is to be expected especially in the acute stage.[17] Adolescents are prone to even more pronounced anger due to the volatility and extremes of their emotional reactions. It is crucial that you not react to this hostility in a personal way. It needs to be viewed as part of the defensive repertoire of bereaved teens that they call on when they otherwise would feel overwhelmed. Clearly, if the anger is out of control and takes the form of verbally abusing the helper or physically lashing out, appropriate limits need to be set in a calm but firm manner. Teens would gain nothing by being allowed to express their anger in an uncontrolled or destructive manner.

Anger is more easily expressed especially for adolescent boys than intense yearning and longing for the deceased parent.[18] It may take the form of angry protest about the loss or it may be a way of attempting to draw attention to the distress they feel. The rage may also serve to punish themselves and others for what has happened. Anger may also be expressed through the mode of depression.[19] Angry withdrawal, sulking, refusal to give, and angry unwillingness to utilize their own resources are all signs of the underlying rage expressed through the faulty interpersonal practices of depression. You should be careful not to reinforce these unhealthy interpersonal responses. In a gentle but firm manner, you need to assist adolescents to see how these reactions are compounding their misery and unhappiness and how they can be changed. This latter point is extremely important because those who develop a depressive pattern experience themselves as hopelessly trapped in a painful way of living but do not see their part in it or any way out of it.

Helping Adolescents Grieve the Death of a Sibling

Strive to maintain or restore the communication, support, and cohesion of the family. Research studies indicate that although adolescent boys and girls often reach out to peers and share many personal matters, the prime confidants for both boys and girls are family members, especially mothers.[20] When a sibling dies, the impact on the family can be so devastating that communication and sharing grinds to a halt and leads to increasing isolation and loneliness of its members.[21]

A very sensitive and moving depiction of this compounded effect of family tragedy can be seen in the film, *The Stone Boy*, in which a school-age child accidently shoots and kills his teenage brother while hunting.[22] The child made several attempts to unburden his intense grief and guilt to his parents but they were too grief-stricken to communicate and share feelings with him. No one in the family was really able to talk about this trauma. Gradually, the youngster spent more and more time away from the home, staying with his grandfather who was very supportive of him but he still could not break the stony silence about his painful sense of loss and guilt. Finally, his agitated, unrelenting, and unspoken grief led him to run away to Las Vegas to see an aunt. After a disappointing visit with his aunt he returned home on a bus. During the bus ride he noticed a woman with a baby crying in back of him. He went back and sat next to her. He broke his silence with this complete stranger. In a very moving scene with many tears he finally shared his heavy oppressive emotional burden.

Families as grief-stricken as the Stone Boy's need help in being able to communicate again, to be able to talk about the deceased sibling, to be able to comfort one another, and gradually to let go by withdrawing their emotional investment in the deceased and moving on with their lives. The family represents the greatest potential healing ally of the helper.

Help the adolescent and family develop realistic time frames and expectations of the grief process. Studies indicate that the bereavement process can easily extend well beyond a year. While many bereaved persons insist that the first year is the roughest, others state that it was the second year that was the hardest. It may be that as time goes on there is less and less social support for grievers as family members and friends expect them to get on with their lives. These well-meaning friends and family members may be laboring under the same misconceptions that many helpers have in the beginning of their work with the bereaved. They may feel it is possible to push people through the stages of grief and shorten the cycle, thereby sparing them prolonged pain. However, these are not realistic expectations and, in fact, will very likely complicate the natural healing process. The pace of change for each griever needs to be respected and appreciated. Sometimes when the bereaved get stuck in certain stages of the grieving process (such as angry unwillingness to let go or move on) confrontation may be needed. It is very important, however, how this is done. If it is done with impatience because the caregiver feels frustrated that the griever is not responding, it will almost surely fail. If it is done firmly but with gentleness, compassion, and true concern for the needs of the griever, it is much more likely to have a beneficial effect. Grievers and helpers alike will benefit from having a realistic time frame for accomplishing the grief work.

One study addressed the effects of the death of a sibling on adolescents.[23] The interviews on the average were held nearly two years after the sibling death. At that point a significant portion of these adolescents (one-third to one-half) were still experiencing symptoms of guilt, loneliness, depression, confusion, and anger. Thus, the experience of bereavement can easily extend beyond the commonly held expectations of griever and helper alike. Certainly, you should not predict it will take two years or more lest it become a self-fulfilling prophecy. It is helpful to tell grievers that it frequently takes longer than most people expect and their own reactions are well within the normal range.

Be alert to previous unresolved losses complicating the grieving process. The current loss of a sibling may resonate with previous losses such as the death of a grandparent or a friend for whom the mourning was incomplete. It is always wise to inquire about such prior losses when undertaking counseling with bereaved adolescents. Teens may be particularly resistant to mourning if it means opening earlier unhealed wounds. A metaphor drawn from physical medicine may be useful here. Just as a broken bone causes momentarily increased pain while being reset, only in so doing is the healing process set in motion. Not to reset the bone properly in order to avoid the temporary intensification of pain would cause far more pain in the long run.

Be sensitive to the special conflicts that can arise for the adolescent whose sibling dies. The intense rivalries that divide siblings can leave a special burden of guilt for bereaved adolescents. A much younger sibling may be resented because of occupying the role of "king baby" in the family. Older siblings may be alternatively admired and envied because of their superior abilities and privileges in the world. Thus, sibling death is often complicated by the competitiveness that frequently characterizes family relationships in our culture. Competitiveness is a major distorting and warping influence on personality development.[24] It tends to breed mistrust and cynicism, which rob human beings of their potential for true intimacy and closeness. It also complicates significantly the grieving process for adolescents who lose a sibling and much attention will need to be directed at helping them resolve their ambivalent feelings.

The loss of an older sibling may also represent the loss of a source of secure identification, someone who could show them the ropes of adult life.[25] Just as sibling rivalry can be intense so can sibling bonds.[26] This is especially true in families where there have been significant stresses and hardships. In such cases, the siblings may feel they owe their survival to the close bond formed with brothers and/or sisters. The death of a sibling can thus be exceedingly painful.

Helping Adolescents Grieve Other Special Losses

While the death of a parent may be the most devastating and the loss of a sibling extremely painful, perhaps the most frequently encountered deaths during adolescence are those of grandparents and pets. Some adolescents may enjoy a very special relationship with grandparents and their death may be very impactful. Those who have grown somewhat distant as a result of their increasing involvement with peers and their own pursuits outside of the family may, nevertheless, remember the special love shared with grandparents at earlier times. Likewise, adolescents sometimes grieve the loss of a family pet just as painfully as younger children. Pets in some families are loved and valued to the extent that their death can trigger a mourning reaction as intense as the loss of a family member, though usually of much shorter duration. For most adolescents these deaths are the first exposure to a significant family loss. Their ability to grieve the loss of a grandparent, or aunt or uncle or even a family pet, can help buffer them from the stressful effects of subsequent deaths that they will inevitably face as they continue through the life cycle.

Adolescents typically form very close relationships with peers. The loss of a boyfriend or girl friend through death has frequently been a theme of adolescent songs. The loss of a love relationship so early in its development and so full of promise represents the ultimate tragedy in the eyes of many. Same sex friendships can also be very intense and the death of a peer at this age can provoke enormous anxiety as adolescents are forced to confront, perhaps as never before, their own mortality and vulnerability. The circumstances of death of a peer can often be sudden and traumatic since the three leading causes of death among adolescents are accidents, suicides, and homicides.

The suicide of a friend can be especially devastating since the "what if" questions are haunting and the accompanying guilt unrelenting. Those helpers working in schools and churches will need to reach out especially at such times to bereaved adolescents. Grieving teens are unlikely to seek counseling on their own but may be suffering greatly from inner pain they cannot easily put into words. They may keep their grief hidden because they are afraid of what the reactions of others would be or because they simply don't know what to do with their grief. It is essential to avoid romanticizing death by suicide and to discourage teens from doing so. It should be emphasized that though such deaths cause immense pain to the survivors, life goes on and that it is tragic that the deceased will not be able to share in it. As previously stated, school systems should have in place plans of action for dealing with such potentially traumatic events (see the Good Grief program in the appendix).

Referring Adolescents for Psychotherapy

As with other ages, the high-risk factors for complicated bereavement include sudden, unexpected deaths, especially deaths caused by accidents, homicide, or suicide, so prevalent in adolescence. In addition, bereavement may be complicated by an excessively dependent or ambivalent relationship with the deceased. Finally adolescents who manifested prior maladjustment such as depression or behavioral difficulties should be considered at risk and may need to be referred for psychotherapy. If adolescents attempt to ward off grief by self-destructive behaviors such as alcohol or drug abuse, or increased thrill seeking or dangerous behavior, they should be referred for individual or family therapy. While it is usually beneficial to involve the whole family in resolving such problems, adolescents will often resist family sessions because it threatens their shaky sense of autonomy. In such cases, it may work better to have individual sessions with adolescents and separate sessions with the parents.

Although the majority of adolescents cope adequately with the stresses of this age, a significant minority are in chronic distress. Manifestations of this disturbance may vary widely and may include depression, anxiety, antisocial behavior, alcohol and drug abuse, runaway behavior, and even suicidal gestures. Chronically distressed youngsters who are then faced with the death of a parent may need to be referred to a mental health professional for psychotherapy since they will likely need more extensive help than can be offered in the context of grief counseling.

Some children may enter adolescence with an underdeveloped sense of self, consisting of fearful and overly compliant patterns of relating to parents. These adolescents may find the process of emancipation from parents and developing an identity of their own especially threatening. Often these youngsters express their conflict about growing up through school underachievement and failure.[27] For them the death of a parent may lead to a severe setback in accomplishing this task of individuation. These adolescents may require a great deal more than bereavement counseling and should be referred for psychotherapy.

The threat of suicide must be carefully considered with adolescents, particularly if accompanied by signs of depression, such as withdrawal, low energy, sadness, loss of appetite, poor concentration, and irritability. In all such cases, referral for a mental health evaluation is recommended. The risk is increased for bereaved adolescents when the death was by suicide. Adolescents are often impulsive and sometimes highly suggestible; these characteristics have led to tragic cases of cluster suicides, in which one suicide in the community trigger others. Schools need to develop a plan of action to assist adolescents in coping with the anxiety, fear, guilt, and pain that such deaths evoke. Schools and churches can develop not only plans to deal with crisis but also educational programs that help to deromanticize suicide as a solution to life problems and help youths develop adaptive alternatives.

Summary

Teens are in the throes of a significant transition. Adolescence is one of the most pivotal developmental stages in the life cycle. Grieving a death in the family or of a peer during this stage of life poses unique challenges. This chapter has discussed developmental considerations, general guidelines in helping bereaved adolescents, and grieving of special losses including the death of a parent, a sibling, and a peer. While death of a significant other is an extremely stressful experience for adolescents, it need not be overwhelming or impede the developmental process. A number of practical suggestions to assist the healthy grieving process were offered. In the next chapter we will begin to examine bereavement through the adult stages of the life cycle.

5

Helping Young Adults to Grieve

The death of a loved one for young adults is often experienced as a cruel and untimely blow as illustrated by the anguishing words of Larry:

> I can't believe she is dead. Two years ago we were married. Now she is gone. We had so many hopes and dreams. I feel completely lost without her. When the resident asked my permission to perform an autopsy on Becky, I felt like punching him in the mouth.
>
> —Larry, age twenty-two

The period of young adult life from approximately twenty to forty-five is a time of moving away from one's family of origin and forming intimate ties. According to Erikson, the developmental crisis of this period is intimacy vs. isolation, that is, the ability to merge one's self with the self of another.[1] Failure to do so results in loneliness and isolation. Erikson believes that real intimacy is only possible after a reasonable sense of identity has been established. The mature love of the young adult goes beyond the adolescent attachment between boy and girl and involves the appreciation of the other as a separate person in the context of a committed relationship. Having achieved this true intimacy the loss of one's life partner can be devastating.

The period before leaving home is a time when we feel protected from life but pay a price in terms of many restrictions. The twenties is the period when we have made the transition out of our families of origin but have not yet established a secure pattern of adult life. Furthermore, in the twenties we feel we have all the time in the world to reach our goals and aspirations. The end of the twenties is a time when choices are becoming more complex and we realize that there is not enough time to pursue all the many pathways leading to our dreams. Then, between the midthirties and midforties, we experience a new sense of time urgency in conjunction with an emotional (not just intellectual) awareness of our own mortality.[2]

According to this developmental scheme, the way time is experienced undergoes gradual transformation from young adulthood to middle age at around forty-five. In the early adult years life seems to offer endless promise with plenty of time to pursue our many dreams. By the end of the decade of the twenties, we realize the need to renounce some of our aspirations because there simply won't be time and energy to pursue let alone fulfill them all. Some of these dreams fall hard. It can be a bitter and disillusioning experience to forfeit cherished hopes and aspirations. It can also be liberating in that it frees energy to pursue what is realistic and possible. By the middle of the next decade of the thirties, the sense of life's finiteness impacts the way we experience time, creating in many a sense of urgency. While this can be viewed as a negative, if we can appreciate the inevitability of our death we are in a far better position to value life.

Given this developmental framework it is easier to appreciate the impact of losses during the early adult years. When one is just beginning to establish intimate ties, the death of a family member is so untimely and enormously painful.

Helping Young Adults Grieve the Loss of a Spouse

The loss of a spouse at any age is extremely painful. To lose a spouse in the early adult years when many dreams and hopes remain unfulfilled is especially hard to accept. The bereavement can especially be complicated when, as in Sally's case, there is considerable dependency on the deceased spouse:

> I feel so confused, helpless, lonely and unable to make decisions since Ken died. I was so dependent on him. I've always had difficulty making decisions. I feel a need to put on a good front for friends and relatives and my child. I feel so scared. He has been gone six months and I haven't been able to dispose of his personal papers or clothing. I can't go to sleep without images of caskets and going into the hospital room.
>
> —Sally, age twenty-six

Much focus in Sally's counseling was on helping her recognize resources she could call on to make a life for herself and her child and to resolve the angry unwillingness that blocked her utilization of these resources. For a long time Sally held onto the fantasy that another man as wonderful as Ken would come along and without any effort or initiative on her part would take over and make everything all right. It also was very difficult for Sally to admit to some angry feelings toward Ken and to acknowledge some disappointments in the marital relationship that had blocked her ability to mourn fully, to let go and move on in her life. Like many others, Sally thought that she shouldn't have such feelings and tenaciously clung to her idealizations of Ken until she was strong enough to face all facets of her feelings. Only then could she achieve a realistic balance between an appreciation of his many good qualities and some of his shortcomings.

Sally also needed to resolve a very painful sense of guilt. The night before Ken's fatal car accident, they had argued. Later that night he wanted to make love and she pushed him aside. He said, "You will be sorry." She fired back, "Just keep your life insurance paid up." She explained, "I never got a chance to apologize or tell him how much I loved him." She also blamed herself for not being more assertive with the doctors at the hospital. She stated, "If they had operated sooner perhaps he could have been saved." Sally did work through her guilt and eventually did meet a man and remarried. On follow-up ten years later she reports being happily married and very invested in her marriage and a career. Her child is now in college and doing well. She sees herself as more independent and more capable of making decisions. She is enjoying meeting new challenges by starting a business of her own. Thus, as painful as the bereavement process is, it sometimes can open the door to growth and healthy personality change.

Assist in making the loss real and concrete. Sometimes this first task of grieving can be accomplished by encouraging a visit to the grave. This visit very often is an important step toward recognizing the reality of the loss. It can help also to talk about the funeral in a detailed manner. Questions such as, what did they like or dislike about the funeral, are intended to help mourners focus on the concrete aspects of death to assist them in emotionally recognizing a reality that intellectually they know has occurred. Gail struggled hard to accept such a reality:

My husband has been dead ten months but I don't like to admit publicly that he is dead. I keep thinking "he's away." I attempt projects but I have no feeling about them. While wallpapering a room I can only think that this is something that Michael and I were going to do together.

—Gail, age thirty-three

Attentive listening and reflective statements such as "Gail, I am sure that you wish more than anything in the world that Michael was 'just away' instead of having died on October nineteenth of last year," can help to validate the intense longing at the same time making the death more real. Death has an actual concrete date on the calendar and referring to it is a way of actualizing the loss.

The importance of this step of making the death concrete is exemplified by the difficulties survivors of victims of plane crashes (where the bodies are not recovered) have in grieving simply because the loss is not real to them. Our need to deny the loss is so powerful that without concrete manifestations and reminders of the death, the process of grieving can be inhibited. Similar blocks to mourning have been noted among the families of servicemen missing in action.

Accompany bereaved young adults as they identify and express the painful emotions of grief. The death of a spouse during the young adult period of life evokes such powerful feelings of all kinds. The horror of untimely death is well expressed by Jim:

When the doorbell rang in the middle of the night I was scared, but my God I couldn't believe the nightmare unfolding before my eyes as the policeman explained my wife had been in a terrible accident and

I had better come to the hospital. When I got there
they wanted me to identify the body. She was so
young. We had so many plans. I am so furious! How
do you accept something like this? I know I will never
be the same again. Oh, how I miss her!

—Jim, age thirty-one

It can be very difficult to accompany someone in such
acute pain without being overwhelmed. Because it is so
heart wrenching there is the temptation to do things to
ease the pain that may interfere with the natural healing
process of identifying, embracing, and sharing these powerful feelings with a trusted person. In the process of
doing so, the griever can learn to bear and tolerate these
feelings. Jim is right, he will never be the same again.
Recovering from bereavement doesn't mean that you return to a preloss state of functioning. Rather, it means
you learn to live with the loss and gradually you become
less preoccupied and able to focus on other things including building a new life. It is important, however, to challenge the myth that time alone is a healer.[3] The bereaved
are often surprised when even years later while watching
television or reading a book they are reminded of their
loss and the pain comes back with startling intensity. As
time passes more and more opportunities present themselves for doing the grief work but if grief is denied or
avoided the mourning may take a distorted form no matter how much time elapses. The work of grief is an active
process of mastery. Time alone will not bring about the
resolution that typically requires the active steps described
in chapter 1.

*It is essential to respect the pace that is appropriate to the
needs of young bereaved adults.* Young adults who have lost
a spouse will find their life circumstances radically altered.

In addition to the painful longing and missing of the loved one, there are the dashed hopes, dreams, and expectations. Suddenly there is no longer the sense of life's great promise and all the time in the world to fulfill it. Rather the uncertainties, vulnerabilities, and limitations of life are agonizingly real. In addition, when a spouse dies, overnight one is either all alone or in charge of a family as a single parent, a lonely and formidable task for even the most loving and committed parent. There may be huge hospital and doctor bills to face. In some cases there will be a need for a surviving spouse to sell a home and find a smaller or less-expensive house or find a better-paying job. With all these changes and adjustments to cope with externally it is no wonder that some pacing is required in order to accomplish the internal work of grieving. The helper will need to assist the bereaved in achieving a balance. An exclusive focus on the internal grief work to be done without attention to the realistic hardships posed by external realities would be extremely shortsighted.

It is crucial to respect the uniqueness of the young adult griever. The bereaved should not be subjected to pressures to follow a prescribed course in facing their grief. They need to feel free to find the ways that are best for them. All of the recommendations in this book must be viewed in this context. While the generalizations about what is helpful may apply to a large number of bereaved persons they will not fit every person and it becomes a very important challenge for the helper to search and explore with the bereaved what is helpful for that specific person or family.

Utilize as fully as possible the resources of the family system. Young adults who have lost a spouse, one of the most painful and stressful experiences in life, will certainly benefit from the love, support, and concern of their extended families. It may be helpful to include members of the

extended family in counseling sessions to solidify the mutual support and caring that can be so sustaining at a
time of severe crisis in the lives of young adults. If the
relationships with extended family are highly conflictual
or distant, severe stresses such as the death of a spouse
may cause even further division. In such cases, the young
adult should be encouraged to turn to those who are emotionally available such as other relatives or close friends.
It needs to be understood by counselors that tragedy does
not bring all families closer together.

Address the loneliness felt by young widows and widowers. One
of the most painful aspects of bereavement for young widows or widowers is the loneliness they feel. Listening empathically during the early months of loss may be the most
helpful thing that you can do. If you begin too early to
encourage new activities and relationships before the
grievers are ready you will be experienced as insentive
and unhelpful. As the months pass, these young adults
will want to resume social participation and dating gradually. After such a painful bereavement many young widows or widowers will be reluctant to invest emotionally
in a new relationship, believing that they could not endure
the pain again if something should happen to the new
person. If they have young children, they may also be
worried about the effects of introducing a new person
into the lives of their children for the same reason. The
children may attempt to sabotage new relationships both
because of fear of making a new attachment and of a
wish not to share their remaining parent with someone
else. You can assist with this transition by offering support
to both parent and children as they open themselves ever
so cautiously to new relationships.

*Be mindful of what bereaved adults have considered as helpful
interactions.* Some very interesting studies of postbereave-
ment adjustment have been performed by Maddison and

colleagues and the outcome was found related to the interactions within their social network.[4] Those widows who had fared poorly shared the following perceptions:

(1) The widows felt they needed more encouragement and support in expressing their emotions, such as grief and anger.

(2) They expressed a need for more opportunity to talk about their husband and their life together.

(3) They needed nonjudgmental acceptance of the expression of their feelings of guilt; this was especially helpful when the relationship had been intensely ambivalent.

(4) These widows also needed support in talking about the negative as well as the positive features of the lost relationship.

(5) They also felt they required more practical help and general support than was available in their social environment.

It is also important to consider those responses that were regarded decidedly unhelpful. Maddison and colleagues also found the following responses from the widow's social environment to be decidedly unhelpful and frequently blocked the widow's ability to grieve:

(1) Showing shock in reaction to the widow's expression of feelings.

(2) Admonishing the widow to control herself and pull herself together.

(3) Recommendations that she think of the suffering of others as a way of minimizing her own grief.

(4) Insisting that she not be angry or guilty.

(5) Advising her not to cry since she would upset others.

(6) Suggesting that she not think of the past but focus on the future.

(7) Recommending that she take up new friendships

or activities or even think of remarriage during the stage
of acute grief.

Many of the above attempts to help by well-meaning
people in the family and social environment stem from
the sense of impotence and helplessness that people tend
to feel when confronted with a person in acute grief. The
tendency is to push the person to do something or to
feel something that is not in keeping with their genuine
needs and feelings. Some of these same suggestions might
be considered helpful at a later point in the sequence
of the grief work. What these studies seem to confirm
is what Bowlby emphasizes when he suggests that we are
far more helpful when we offer to be a companion to
accompany the bereaved through their journey of grief
rather than being eager to take on the role of being a
representative of reality.[5] Other studies have shown that
where the social environment was inadequate in providing
the needed support for the bereaved, counseling interventions in the form of supportive interactions that encourage
the bereaved to mourn is likely to markedly improve outcome.[6]

It is important to be aware of sex role influences. While bereaved young mothers and widows in Western cultures
are typically supported in the open expression of their
sadness and longing through words and tears, men usually
feel inhibited in such expressions lest it appear unmanly.
Thus, men will usually require explicit and direct encouragement to grieve but are certainly capable of doing so
when given the proper support. One man stated, "All
my life I have ignored and pushed away my feelings; now
the feeling side of my self is demanding equal time." If
ever the feeling side of men needs attention and encouragement of expression, it is when a wife or child has died.

Do not let cultural stereotypes lead you to feel that only women will make good use of grief counseling.

Be aware of critical periods and anniversary reactions. Certain points in time seem harder than others in the grief process, and those doing grief counseling need to be aware of them and to make contact with the bereaved if there is no regular ongoing relationship. One such point is three months after the death of the loved one.[7] Immediately after the death the support of family and friends is at a peak and the shock and denial may also be intense. As time passes the need for others to return to their normal pattern of life intensifies along with the loneliness and sense of isolation of the bereaved. Thus, three months after the death may be a particularly hard time for the grieving person and a good time for the helper to be in touch. Anniversaries of the death, especially the first one, are often another critical time along with the birthday of the deceased person and, of course, holidays and special family occasions like weddings and christenings. It is sometimes helpful to anticipate with the bereaved that these will be difficult times, and, if they are dreading events such as the holidays, to engage in some advance planning that enables them to feel some sense of mastery and control in the situation. These special times also represent an opportunity for further grief work in the form of expressing and sharing feelings with others who share their pain and care about them. For those who lack the supportive network of family and friends to share such events, the mutual help and support groups available in most communities will offer an alternative. The bereavement support groups may be very beneficial even to those fortunate bereaved young adults with a supportive and caring network of family and friends. They offer the opportunity to share one's grief with others who have gone through similar losses. Even in the most understanding families there may be a tendency to hurry along the process of grief so as to shorten the period of agony and pain. Those who have experienced it will appreciate that you cannot go around grief but rather you have to go through it.

Helping Young Adults Grieve the Death of a Child

Losing a child, especially a young child, is the most painful and stressful experience in life. Young adult parents experience an extreme emotional upheaval and frequently feel they are losing their minds. They typically experience significant somatic distress, including tightness of chest, rapid breathing, and digestive distress along with loss of appetite and interest in usual activities. They find it hard to concentrate and remember things, and are subject to extreme mood swings and deep depression. These are all normal manifestations of acute grief.

Whether the child dies from an accident or from some form of illness, it is a traumatic experience: young children are not supposed to die. Parents do not expect to have to bury their children. It is not in the natural order to do so. Deaths of children through accidents or illness can be devastating to the whole family. Where death comes slowly through illnesses such as leukemia, the family's hopes rise and fall based on the latest lab test results and the apparent response to the latest treatment. Then there may be a period of remission when the family members feel that they are finally out of the woods only to be followed sometimes years later by the grim, heartbreaking news of relapse. The following are examples of expressions of the almost-indescribable pain experienced by young bereaved parents:

He was the joy of our lives. How do you accept the death of a child? He was only four. How can a child this young get so sick and die when he was so full of life and love? Our pain is almost unbearable. I am certain of one thing, we'll never be the same again.

—Beth, age twenty-four, and Michael, age twenty-six

I relive over and over the ambulance coming to the house and taking my baby away. It was the most horrible moment of my life. My baby wasn't breathing. My God! I still don't believe it. I loved her so very much!

—Elizabeth, age thirty-one

In the case of fatal accidents, murder, and suicide of a child, the grief is compounded by the sudden horror of these events and the rage "that something like this could happen to our child." The guilt can also be nearly unbearable, particularly in the case of childhood suicide, but also with accidents to the extent that they are perceived as preventable.

These families will need someone who can sit with them and listen intently and patiently to their grief and share their pain. Of course we cannot share their pain fully, and we should be honest in acknowledging that we can't fully appreciate what it is like for them to lose a child. They will have to teach us what it is like for them. Yet as we sit with more and more parents grieving such painful losses, we realize that we do have something to offer. For one thing, we come to feel with conviction that they will survive even though they probably don't think they will at the time. Our belief and faith that even nearly unbearable grief can be borne and find resolution may provide hope at a time when so little is experienced by the grief-stricken parents. Our ability to hear their pain empathically without becoming overwhelmed ourselves may enable them to gather the strength to tolerate these most painful of feelings. Their anger and outrage are likely to be intense, but if they can frame both into words they are much less likely to overwhelm them or be expressed in destructive forms.

The intensity of the bereavement may lead to failure and breakdown in the family and social support system. Extended family and friends may find that their own pain over the loss of the child leads them to withdraw. The parents may feel angry and disappointed regarding these responses and turn to professionals who may also find it painful to accompany them on the long road to recovery. These parents sometimes find that they gain the greatest support by turning to others who have shared similar experiences such as Compassionate Friends, a mutual-help group for bereaved parents (see appendix for address). At times the distress experienced by helpers stems largely from the sense of impotence and helplessness. In this book there has been much emphasis on what as helpers we can do. One thing we can't do is take away the pain of a parent such as Joan in the following example who has lost a much loved child:

> I couldn't stop screaming. "It's my baby your talking about! It's my baby! What do you mean, he is dead! I still don't want to believe it."
>
> —Joan, age twenty-five

We can, however, accompany them as they share their feelings so that they are not alone in their pain. By our willingness to hear and explore their feelings they gradually learn to tolerate and to live with these previously nearly unbearable and overwhelming emotions of grief.

Help the bereaved young parents to acknowledge and resolve ambivalence. Given how very painful the loss of a child is for young adults, it may be especially difficult for them to acknowledge ambivalence. Yet it is hard to imagine that one could care for a child without some negative and perhaps even hateful feelings developing at times. A baby crying night after night cannot help but be enraging to even the most devoted sleep-deprived parents. Such negative feelings when unacknowledged can block the mourning process. You should expect that such feelings will not be shared until a considerable degree of trust has been built through the counseling relationship. Normalizing such ambivalent feelings, however, may open the door to the ability of the bereaved to be able to share such feelings of their own. In counseling couples who have lost a child it may be especially hard for either parent to admit in front of the other such hostile feelings toward their deceased child but often when one risks it both feel a considerable sense of relief. They then no longer feel alone in having such feelings and also start to realize that maybe they are not such terrible people for having these feelings in the first place. Once they have been able to articulate fully the hostile and other negative feelings toward their dead child, it is important to remind them of their loving feelings so as to help them achieve an appropriate sense of balance and perspective regarding their feelings. A frequent indication of incomplete mourning is the idealizations so commonly expressed about the child who has died.[8] These idealizations if not gradually relinquished for an appreciation of the child's real nature can lead to unfavorable comparisons to the other children in the family or to seeking a replacement child.[9]

Participate as a member of a team and be knowledgeable about religious, community, and professional resources. No one helper can be expected to provide for all the needs of a grief-stricken young couple who have lost a baby. You need to know about support groups for bereaved parents within the community. These mutual help and support groups offer distinct advantages and benefits. Bereaved persons have the opportunity to share their feelings and experiences with others who have gone down the same painful road and have managed to survive. It is important to recognize when the family's minister, priest, or rabbi can be helpful in offering religious support and spiritual guidance. You need to be alert to possible medical problems requiring the attention of the family physician such as inadequate nutrition, chronic lack of sleep, or frequent minor illnesses. It is vital to recognize when referral to a mental health professional for psychotherapy is needed because the grief is complicated or blocked and taking an unhealthy or distorted path. It is essential to be aware of national organizations that can provide useful information and assistance to the bereaved facing special losses. A number of these organizations and their addresses are listed in the appendix.

When a young mother miscarries, do not underestimate the grief and sense of personal loss. Research has shown that maternal grief for a miscarriage is as intense as for a stillborn or neonatal death.[10] The special meaning and significance of the pregnancy to the couple need to be explored since this will influence the intensity of their grief.[11] The grief may be intense as the mother mourns the loss of the cherished, longed-for child. She may also grieve without wide social support because a pregnancy lost in the early stages may be unannounced and poorly recognized by others. Support groups such as SHARE may be very beneficial (see appendix for address).

If the miscarriage terminates a long-sought and desired

pregnancy or one of a series of attempts to bear a child there may be intense feelings of guilt and personal failure. Guilt may be especially strong if ambivalent feelings about the pregnancy reached the point of considering abortion. The couple will need to talk about their intense sadness, their anger, their guilt, the cherished lost hopes and dreams. Their grief may be especially intense around and during the originally projected due date and the couple may need added support at that point.

The father's sadness may also be intense. If it is a first pregnancy or if it brings to mind prior losses that were not fully mourned the father may also experience acute grief. With the father as well as the mother it would be important to pursue the meaning of the pregnancy and the significance of the loss in order to understand his grief. In any case, since the mother will benefit greatly from the empathic support and understanding of her husband it would be preferable to do grief counseling with the couple together. This will reinforce their emotional ties as they share this intense experience of personal loss. As in all cases of the loss of a child, if the couple decides to have another child, they should be encouraged to appreciate the specialness of the new child and not think of him/her as a replacement for the lost child.[12]

Be aware of the complex issues pertaining to grief resulting from an induced abortion. To the extent that the decision to terminate a pregnancy is perceived as being forced on the young woman by others or medical or economic necessities, the abortion may represent a significant personal loss to be grieved. There may be very little social support for such grieving since those who strongly advocated the abortion will insist that the woman should feel relief. The guilt for some women will be intense because, depending on their religious, cultural, and family values, they may equate on either a conscious or an unconscious level the abortion with murder.[13] The more ambivalent the decision and the less the social support for expressing such highly conflicted feelings, the more likely the grief will take a delayed or distorted form.

The role of the father of the baby in influencing the outcome of the grief process may be crucial. Some fathers who have mutually agreed on the termination of the pregnancy will nevertheless experience intense loss or guilt and these feelings need to be recognized and worked through. Some fathers will be angry and unsupportive of the abortion; in this case the grief process for both is likely to be complicated. Seeing the couple together in grief counseling may offer the opportunity to work through some of the conflictual feelings. Failure to mourn fully the loss and conflictual feelings surrounding abortion may lead to other unwanted pregnancies. Such unplanned pregnancies and repeated abortions are particularly likely in the young unmarried group.[14]

According to Theresa Rando, the proportion of women who experience significant postabortion stress is relatively small (she estimates no more than 10 percent).[15] Rando states that only 1 percent of those selecting abortions will have chronic grief, guilt, or depression that significantly interferes with their ability to function.

It is crucial for those assisting the grief of parents who are terminating pregnancies to examine their own feelings and reactions to abortion. Some counselors may not be able to do this kind of grief work because of deeply held religious values or personal convictions and will need to refer to other helpers. If we do seek to help young people facing this loss we will need to monitor continuously our own conflicts and ambivalence about abortion so that we can respond in a helpful and empathic manner.

Be sensitive to factors that interfere with grieving for a still-

birth. Expectant mothers who go through nine months of pregnancy only to deliver unexpectedly a dead baby experience an acute sense of loss. The grief of fathers is often neglected but can also be intense. Once again, it is advisable to take a family-systems perspective and meet with the couple together in grief counseling and include any children in the family who may also be experiencing a sense of loss. Sometimes the stillbirth is expected and anticipatory grieving begins prior to the delivery. In these instances going through the painful process of labor can be all the more difficult for the mother. A number of factors have been identified as interfering with grieving for a stillborn child:[16]

(1) The mother being heavily sedated;
(2) Prevention of the parents from seeing the baby;
(3) Inability of the parents to communicate and share their grief;
(4) A previously poor self-image for the mother;
(5) A lack of support in the social environment.

Given these factors influencing outcome, you should focus on bolstering the self-esteem of the mother; encourage interactions with significant others whose support is critical; work with the family system so as to facilitate communication and sharing of grief; and advocate for the couple who wish to see their stillborn baby.

Validate the grief of parents who grieve for the loss of a newborn child. Although they may have had limited opportunities to develop an attachment to their sick or premature baby, the loss is very real and painful. When death occurs suddenly and unexpectedly to neonates who have appeared healthly, the sense of shock, numbness, and denial can be great. Research and clinical experience point to the value of the parents being allowed to hold the baby immediately after death. They need to understand the cause of death and its significance regarding risks to subsequent children. They will need to talk about the baby, the pregnancy, their hopes, their expectations, and their terrible sense of loss over and over again. As in all sudden deaths, anger is likely to be prominent among the emotions deeply felt and will need ample opportunities for expression. Again, fathers should not be overlooked as they too may experience acute grief, especially if they were involved in the care of the infant.

Be sensitive to the special issues related to Sudden Infant Death Syndrome (SIDS). This baffling syndrome that has no known definite explanation is a leading cause of death of infants between one week and one year of age in the United States. These sudden unexplained deaths occur to apparently healthy infants, usually while the child is asleep. Postmortem examinations do not reveal any typical accepted cause of death.[17] These losses can be especially traumatic for young adult couples. Many of these couples after such a traumatic experience find it next to impossible to sleep at night if they have a subsequent baby. The deaths are sudden and unexplained leading to shock and often guilt and self-blame. Since the feelings of helplessness and powerlessness are so painful to tolerate the tendency is to blame oneself or in the case of couples to sometimes blame each other. This, of course, can lead to a major marital crisis since the death of a child under any circumstances is extraordinarily stressful, but under these conditions even more so. The stress may be compounded by insinuations from family, friends, or neighbors that perhaps the parents had failed to exercise proper care of the infant. It is absolutely critical that helpers don't add to the enormous burden of guilt and self-blame that these couples experience. One of the most helpful interventions may be to assist the couple in obtaining sound information to allay the "if onlys" that so frequently plague these young parents.[18] You may not be able to address all of these concerns but you can direct the couple to medical professionals, the National SIDS Foundation (see appendix), and support groups that can provide both considerable information and support.

If the baby lost to SIDS is the couple's first child there may be an especially painful sense of failure related to the many self-doubts and insecurities that new parents typically experience. The understanding and support of the extended family and friends will be enormously helpful to the young adults in their recovery. You may be able to facilitate communication within the support network so as to reinforce these crucial connecting links. It is important that the grief-stricken couple not be isolated and cut off from others although their sense of guilt and self-blame may lead them to seek such distance. Understandably they will also need their privacy and solitude, so you may be able to assist them in achieving a balance in keeping with their genuine needs. It is a very sad and heartbreaking experience to sit with a young couple grieving for the loss of what they viewed as their healthy baby.

Helping young people through their intense grief and pain requires that you take care of yourself. You will need the support and caring of your own family, interests and hobbies, recreational outlets, and professional support to sustain you for the important and meaningful work you do. While this is true for all helpers working with the bereaved it is especially true of those who help parents grieve for the loss of a child because research has demonstrated that this is the most stressful bereavement of all. You cannot be truly committed and fully involved in this work without being deeply touched and moved by the pain of others.

If it begins to overwhelm you, however, then you know it is time to take care of yourself or else you will not be able to help others.

Other Significant Losses

The death of a parent during the early adult stage can be especially devastating. The loss hits hard because young adults may not be firmly established in a secure pattern of life and the encouragement and support of their parents are still very much needed. In addition, there may be considerable unfinished business to be resolved between the young adult and parent. The death of the parent sometimes occurs just at the point when the young adult is getting to know the parent in a new way. They may have begun to relate in an adult-to-adult way for the first time. In addition to the intensely painful sense of personal loss, young people may also mourn the loss of opportunities for the parent to see grandchildren grow up and for their own children to know and love the grandparent.

The death of a sibling during young adulthood can shatter the assumptions so common to this stage that life holds unlimited promise and there is all the time in the world to actualize it. As with other ages the death of a sibling, and particularly of a twin, greatly heightens their sense of vulnerability and personal awareness of death. The bereavement may be especially painful for those siblings who have enjoyed a close bond in their adult years. The grieving process is often complicated by rivalries and resentments that were never resolved between the siblings. The sense of loss may be profound for those siblings who looked after each other as a result of extreme family stressors such as poverty or abuse during the growing-up years.

The death of a friend can be not only a profound personal loss but deeply disturbing to the young adult. When a peer dies it is much harder to maintain the illusions so common to the young-adult stage. Instead of life representing endless promise and time, the personal awareness of death is suddenly and dramatically brought into focus. Friends are extremely important at any stage of the life cycle, but they play a special role during the early adult years in terms of providing support as young adults attempt to establish themselves into a secure pattern of adult life. The death of a friend can result in profound sorrow for young adults.

Referring Young Bereaved Adults for Psychotherapy

In some extremely conflictual marital relationships or where there has been either verbal or physical battering suffered by the surviving spouse, you may find it difficult to assist the bereaved in recovering happy and positive memories and feelings because any review of the past may bring up the painful abusive incidents and it may not be possible to get past these. Some of the most complicated bereavements in my clinical experience have been characterized by such histories. Many of these young adults will need to be referred for intensive psychotherapy since the abusive experiences often create such intense rage that death wishes are almost universal. These wishes contribute to the inordinate burden of guilt felt by survivors along with their inability to recall loving feelings toward the spouse because of the memory inhibition caused by the traumatic abusive events.

While the loss of a child or a spouse is extraordinarily stressful and almost unbearably painful, most young adults survive it. Only a small portion will need to be referred for psychotherapy. As with other ages those at high risk for complicated bereavement will be those with excessively dependent or conflictual relationships with the deceased and when the circumstances of the death are traumatic.

Summary

Young adult life is a time of great hope and promise. Death of a loved one at this stage of life can be a shattering experience. This chapter has examined the impact of special losses on young adults. The deaths of a child and a spouse were emphasized since these bereavements are often the most painful and stressful of all. Guidelines were offered to assist in planning practical interventions for various special losses including miscarriage, stillbirth, neonatal death, abortion, and SIDS. Research has shown that widowhood is especially painful when it occurs in young adult life when it is not expected and there is little emotional preparation for it. Suggestions for helping young adults grieve this devastating loss were given. In addition, the losses of parents, siblings, and friends were considered. In the next chapter the impact of loss on midlife adults will be explored.

6

Helping Adults in Midlife to Grieve

In midlife we begin to look forward to slowing the pace and enjoying the rewards of earlier toils and sacrifices. When death claims a loved one in this stage of life it can be a staggering and exceedingly painful blow as expressed by William:

She collapsed on the floor in the kitchen on Christmas eve. Two days later she died. After thirty-one years of marriage, it's so hard to get used to the empty house. She hadn't been feeling well for several days; I should have insisted she see a doctor sooner. I go over and over it in my mind especially at night. I hardly sleep and its been six weeks since she died. Sometimes I get angry with the doctor, sometimes at the hospital, sometimes at myself and even sometimes at Evelyn for dying. We had such wonderful plans. Our children are grown and the mortgage is paid off and I'd retire in two years. It's not supposed to happen like this.

—William, age fifty-three

During the middle years of adult life, people tend to

reach their prime. People who shall succeed in their careers, business, or in raising a family will show clear evidence of this by their forties. This is the time when parents are reaching old age and children are entering adulthood and getting ready to leave home. Many adults in their forties and fifties experience the death of their parents; this highlights ever more vividly our own mortality because we realize we are next in line to die.[1] Both our parents and our children are undergoing major transitions in their lives. Our parents enter their retirement and declining years and our children begin to make a life and a family of their own. These major shifts by the preceding and succeeding generations can have a deeply unsettling effect on the midlife adult, because the family constellation is undergoing radical transformation. Erik Erikson describes the developmental task of mature adulthood as generativity versus stagnation.[2] Generativity represents the concern for establishing and guiding the next generation. Thus, it represents a wish to impart parental values and attitudes and wisdom to the next generation.

During our forties and fifties our graying and receding hair and wrinkling skin don't allow us to continue to view ourselves as young. Many adults during this period of life frantically try to deny this through various compulsive pursuits designed to stave off the natural aging process. It is also a period of intense questioning. Everything is subjected to intense scrutiny and examination, including our careers, our marriages, the purpose and meaning of our lives. There is also a renewed sense of time urgency as our own personal death appears on the horizon and we begin to view our lives as coming to a close in the distant but foreseeable future. Awareness of personal mortality seems to undermine the immunity pact that men make with work.[3] This pact, usually unconscious, implies that if we work hard and are successful we shall never feel like small, helpless little boys again, and the prospect of our death is diminished in some magical way.

Some of our peers begin to succumb to heart attacks and other fatal diseases along with our parents and we begin to question if this is all there is to life. Attending the funeral of a midlife peer drives home in an emotionally vivid way that we only get one life and raises questions as to whether we are living it the way we really want to. During midlife women who have been the primary nurturers of their families may wish to pursue careers and women who have reached a pinnacle of success in their occupations may wish to focus their concerns more on family or other interests in their life.

Marriage contracts may be questioned, reexamined, and renegotiated in midlife or if the relationship cannot tolerate such examination it might end. If growth isn't accommodated in the relationship, the couple may pay a huge price in resentment even if they decide to stay together. Our definition of happiness and success and the manner in which we evaluate our self-worth may all be called into question during midlife. Deeply held beliefs, attitudes about self and others formed in our developmental years within our original families, are subjected to intense and agonizing scrutiny.

One writer on midlife has described it as the time in life when "the individual has stopped growing up and has begun to grow old."[4] It is the fact of death at the conscious level instead of being a general conception that is the central and crucial aspect of the midlife phase. This is not knowledge of someone else's death but an appreciation of our own very real mortality. This developmental stage of adult life calls for us to make write-offs as we realize we cannot do all that we have set out to do and that so much will remain as works in progress. Our hopes and dreams have to be readjusted and some of our aspirations renounced as our time is more limited than we ever appreciated before. In this developmental context, we must help the bereaved to face their losses.

Death of Adolescent Children

For midlife parents the death of a child usually means the loss of an adolescent or young adult son or daughter. Since adolescents tend to die under sudden and often violent circumstances, the bereavement may be complicated by the unexpected and often traumatic circumstances of the death. The tragedy is particularly difficult to assimilate since adolescents haven't yet had the chance to make a life of their own. Such was the case with the painful bereavement of Marilyn:

> I couldn't believe what they were saying. I just wanted to scream. It can't be true, Oh God! Please say it's not true. My son is too young to die. He hasn't lived yet!
>
> —Marilyn, age forty-five, mother of a sixteen-year-old killed in an alcohol-related car accident.

Help the family achieve a balance between expressing their intense grief and distancing from it. The Harvard Bereavement Study emphasizes that with sudden, unexpected deaths people tend to alternate between expressions of their acute distress and efforts to avoid reminders of their intense pain.[5] As in bereavement with all ages recognition of the reality of the loss is the first step to complete followed by the expression of the emotions of grief. It is important to support detachment and distraction when the painful feelings threaten to overwhelm the bereaved simply because the shock and the pain are too much to assimilate, except in a gradual fashion. When the feelings of grief are too overpowering for the grievers then it becomes important to focus on ways of strengthening the ego. This would include building and enhancing self-esteem, identifying, highlighting, and reinforcing existing defenses, and modeling and teaching of other defenses and adaptive coping skills. *The key is to move the focus away from the direct expression of feelings until the bereaved are strong enough to bear them.*

Be aware that the bereavements of parents are often complicated because of the ambivalence deriving from the adolescent's struggle for autonomy. Especially during early adolescence, when the early volleys are fired in the adolescent battle for autonomy, the relationship with parents may be highly conflictual. If death occurs during this period, anger and guilt are likely to interfere with the grieving process. The bereaved parents may need specific encouragement to grieve since their grief may be blocked by the ambivalence. They will also need to acknowledge the ambivalence and achieve the eventual resolution of the conflictual feelings by striking a proper balance between the warm, loving feelings and the angry, hostile feelings.

Recognize that bereavement is also likely to be complicated when the deceased adolescent had a particular mission in the family. Some teens serve as a focal point in the struggle between two conflicting spouses. The marital conflict is detoured through the teen and the adolescent's troubles or acting out serves to stabilize the marriage. The death of such an adolescent can be expected to have a destabilizing effect on the family system beyond the stress and possible trauma of the death itself. Other teens might have been a favorite of one of the parents and their death may cause that parent enormous pain and maybe rage. The anger may be toward the adolescent who deserted the parent through death. But, the rage may also be directed at the spouse, particularly if he/she does not grieve openly, and at the other children for not being the favored child and yet surviving. Two popular films in recent years poignantly depicted this compounded family tragedy, *Ordinary People*[6] and *Stand by Me*.[7] In both films a teenage son is tragically killed in an accident. In *Ordinary People,* the son who died is the mother's favorite and in *Stand by Me* the father's favorite. Both deceased adolescents are survived by younger brothers who felt resented and guilty for their survival and very much alienated from the parent whose grief is most unresolved.

In families where conflict before the death was intense it can be expected that the death instead of pulling family members together may have the effect of creating even more divisiveness. You will need to address actively the dysfunctional hierarchy so typically manifested in such conflicted and chaotic family situations. An example of a dysfunctional hierarchy would be a family where the parents have abdicated their executive roles. The power in the family is in the hands of the children who simply don't know what to do with it, and are very anxious. In such a family I would try to empower the parents by recognizing their leadership and authority in the family. In a time of family crisis, it is important to get the parents to combine strength and to provide leadership to the family; you should do everything possible to support this parental collaboration. Thus, highlighting and reinforcing generational boundaries can greatly reduce chaos and anxiety in a family that would otherwise compound and complicate the bereavement process.

Death of Adult Children

Although adult children will typically have moved out of the home and achieved a degree of separation from the original family, the death of a son or daughter of any age is still an extremely stressful and painful experience. The meaning of the loss for the parent will have a significant effect on bereavement and should be explored in detail. So often these deaths that violate the natural order of family losses come in an untimely and sudden way. The usual pattern of early shock and numbness is followed by the intense pain of mourning. These deaths are likely to lead to complicated bereavement to the extent that they are sudden and untimely, or that the relationships between the deceased son or daughter and the parent(s) are characterized by either excessive dependency or ambivalence.

Also, at high risk will be those bereaved parents who exhibit characteristics associated with depressive personality. The differential counseling response to these patterns of complicated bereavement will be described in detail later in this chapter in relation to the death of a spouse. Where the relationship between parents and adult children has been highly conflictual or the dependency extreme such as when adult children sacrifice their autonomy to care for an ailing parent or stay at home because of crippling fears of making a life of their own, it is very likely that extensive psychotherapy will be needed.

Other factors such as economic burdens assumed by the parents related to the son or daughter's death, added responsibilities for the care of the grandchildren, conflicts with the son or daughter's surviving spouse and family—all can greatly exacerbate the painful grieving process. Maybe most difficult of all is a situation in which the parents are faced with multiple losses such as in an auto accident or plane crash when several family members are killed.

When midlife brings into focus so many questions about the meaning and purpose of life, it is no wonder that the death of children or other loved ones during this developmental period can have such a devastating effect. It should be kept in perspective, however that the vast majority of people survive midlife, crisis or not, and the painful bereavement process as well.

Death of a Spouse

The death of a spouse at any age or stage in life is one of the most emotionally difficult and taxing experiences of anyone's lifetime. One widower expressed his anguish over the loss of his wife as follows:

> The first two months all I could think about was Millie. We were married for twenty-eight years. We did everything together and I feel totally lost without her. At first, I wanted to die myself. Now I think I can survive but some days I wonder.
>
> —Henry, age fifty-seven

Whether a midlife widow or widower watches a long-time companion gradually suffer and die from a terminal illness or receives that dreaded call indicating that an accident has claimed the life of an intimate partner, the suffering is enormous. Midlife couples have usually shared many years together, often will have raised a family and may have struggled financially during the heavy obligation years of young and middle adult life. When death takes a midlife spouse there may be feelings of tremendous outrage that both the deceased mate and surviving spouse have been cheated out of their hard-earned reward of an easier life following the struggles to raise a family, establish a career, and assure economic security. An example of such shattered dreams and hopes follow:

> We raised five boys and sometimes during their adolescent years I wondered if we were going to last. We have college expenses behind us now and we were so looking forward to enjoying life together. Our youngest son was a senior the year the diagnosis was made. I remember screaming at the doctor, "How can Fred have cancer? He's never been sick in his whole life!" I keep hoping when I wake up the whole thing will just be a bad nightmare but then I open my eyes and I realize that Fred has been dead for five months and I'm just going to have to accept it.
>
> —Aretha, age fifty-seven

The "immunity pact" as previously described, has been violated.[8] This can be a very bitter experience and may lead to many shattered assumptions about life and one's place in the world. At the very least it is likely to intensify the questioning and reexamination of the significance of one's life so common to midlife.

Respond differentially, based on an assessment of the complicating factors in the grief. The Harvard Bereavement Study identified three patterns that places bereaved people at risk for poor outcomes.[9]

They are sudden and unexpected death, an ambivalent relationship with the deceased, and a dependent relationship with the deceased. Research and clinical experience also suggest that these different types of bereavement need to be responded to differently. *Failing to do so may make things worse.*

Those midlife people faced with the unexpected and sudden death of a spouse may not be able to grieve because of the shock, disbelief, and numbness; the expected concomitants of post-traumatic stress disorder. They will not be able to begin the healing process until they have recognized the reality of their loss. Because of frequent opportunities to share their shock and disbelief about what has happened, the denial begins to give way and they are confronted with the painful emotions of grief. Sometimes, the feelings of sadness, longing and yearning, guilt and anger will be too intense for the griever to integrate. When this happens you need to shift to an ego-strengthening approach to allow the bereaved time to gradually master the overpowering feelings.

Midlife widows and widowers who had highly ambivalent and conflictual relationships with their spouses may also be inhibited in grieving. The negative side of the ambivalent feelings may cause mourners so much guilt they avoid all feelings. All relationships are ambivalent to a degree. No one has only loving feelings for an intimate partner of any duration or only hateful feelings either. If, however, the relationship has been highly conflictual, the griever will be at risk for poor outcome. These highly ambivalent mourners can be helped the most by encouraging and eliciting the feelings of grief early on in the bereavement process. Research has shown that, if they do not allow themselves to grieve then, they tend to be in considerable emotional distress a year after the death.[10] It is unlikely that they will acknowledge their ambivalent feelings until they have developed a trusting relationship with you. You may be able to facilitate their sharing such feelings by discussing the ambivalent feelings in relationships as normal and to be expected.

In addition to acknowledging the opposing feelings within themselves, ambivalent bereaved widows and widowers need to achieve some balance between the negative and positive feelings. *They can best reach this resolution through encouragement to articulate both sides of the ambivalence.* As this is done repeatedly, what is frequently described as "the war inside" becomes externalized. This enables the griever to achieve a sense of objectivity and balance with respect to these feelings. When these opposing sets of feelings battle within, the mourner frequently describes confusion and inability to sort out such intense, conflicting emotions. The very process of putting these feelings into words often brings a new perspective. Then, sharing these feelings with a trusted person furthers the healing process.

Often I have had the experience of a bereaved widow or widower in midlife who shares with me the enormous sense of relief that is felt when one is finally able to talk about these conflicting feelings that have raged within since the death of a spouse. He/she describes the sense of shame and guilt that he/she could not feel wholehearted love for the dead husband or wife. He/she was unable to tell anyone about these feelings, and even had difficulty *admitting* to the feelings.

Sometimes the intensely conflictual relationship will call for intensive psychotherapy beyond the scope of grief counseling; referral should be made to a mental health professional. Such a referral may be especially needed, if aside from the ambivalent relationship with the deceased spouse, the surviving widow or widower is a dependent personality, the circumstances of the death were sudden and traumatic, or the social support network is inadequate.

You will need to provide a gentle but firm push to those midlife grievers who were excessively dependent on their deceased spouses. These grievers are likely to manifest the same dependency and pseudohelplessness with you that they displayed to their spouses. Keep in mind that often the perceived help-lessness is a myth that was perpetuated by the collusion of the two spouses. In order for one partner to appear strong and independent, the other partner might have been compelled to appear weak and helpless. Sometimes, the partner who throughout the marriage appeared weak and helpless starts to show surprising strength when the spouse dies.

In other cases, the dependent, helpless orientation stems primarily from the long-standing personality patterns of the griever that were further reinforced by the interactions of the couple. This pattern of personality functioning has been described by Bonime as the underlying core of depression.[11] Those who manifest certain elements in their personality functioning tend to find themselves trapped in a very painful way of living that is often labeled depression. Bonime views this not as an illness but a consequence of faulty and unhealthy ways of relating to others.

Among the elements of depressive personality delineated by Bonime are: (1) manipulativeness; (2) aversion to influence; (3) an unwillingness to give gratification; (4) hostility; (5) anxiety; and (6) despair. Bonime believes the affective core of depression to be rage. This hostility derives from the sense of having missed what Bonime calls nonobligating solicitude or unconditional love in the early years of life. Having missed out on what they needed early on, these individuals experience life with a sense of deprivation and rage. It can never be made up to them, since even if unconditional love were offered in later life (a rare occurrence) it would still not supply the same need because the person receiving it is no longer a child.

Thus, the depressive lives in an environment of what Bonime describes as cumulative deprivation. Whatever is given is always experienced by the depressive as one more increment of "not enough." This further intensifies the underlying rage that is expressed through the mode of depression. As Bonime points out, some people express rage with a shout and others express it by stony silence. Depressives because of their rage at missing out become masters at manipulating others often through pseudo-helplessness. They wage a constant battle against the use of their own resources. The feeling seems to be that "since I didn't get what I needed how can you expect me to gratify you or make a life of my own?"

In the Harvard Bereavement Study, it was noted that those who were excessively dependent on their deceased spouses might have gotten worse when bereavement counseling solely focused on getting them to express their grief.[12] Consistent with Bonime's work in psychotherapy with depressives, the Harvard study found that to help this group you had to confront their helpless and dependent orientations and firmly encourage them to begin to use their resources to move forward with their lives. Some bereaved widows and widowers in this group with excessively dependent and manipulative personalities will need intensive psychotherapy and a referral should be made to a mental health professional. One important diagnostic clue as to whether psychotherapy will be needed, is the response of the bereaved when you point out their strengths and positive resources. Those bereaved persons who manifest excessive dependency because of mistaken beliefs and myths about their role definition in the marriage will respond favorably and will be encouraged by such affirmation of their strengths. Those bereaved persons whose excessive dependency is rooted more in their personalities will respond negatively and very likely with rage to the identification of their strengths. Their typical way of relating is to command the resources of others and to fight against the utilization of their own.

Often, in the background of depressives, a lifelong pattern of underachievement can be discerned. They have had much practice in warding off the influence of others. They behave as though being influenced by others would represent a competitive defeat. When people with this personality pattern experience the death of a spouse in midlife, helpers will find it a formidable challenge to aid them in the bereavement process. They tend to express the emotions of grief quite readily and intensely. They get stuck, however, in the stages of letting go and moving on. Letting go is extremely difficult for them, because the deceased spouse represented someone they could manipulate through their pseudoweakness and helplessness. Thus, the death of a spouse represents far more than the loss of a significant person in their life. It represents a significant threat to their characteristic way of functioning, *to their sense of self.* This is why grief counseling is likely to be ineffective and more intensive psychotherapy is needed with widows and widowers presenting this preexisting personality pattern.

When trying to help the bereaved person with chronic dependency it is important that an emphasis be placed on forward movement, to prevent chronic grief. This can be done by engaging the bereaved in planning their life and setting goals; start with modest, achievable goals and build on that success to tackle more challenging tasks. Homework assignments between counseling sessions would further heighten the responsibility the bereaved widow or widower must assume to go forward with his/her life. It would be important to insist firmly that these assignments be carried out and to take quite seriously any failure to do so. Much can be learned from exploring the reasons behind the failure as illustrated by the case of Beverly.

Beverly was forty-six when her husband died of a heart

attack. During the months following his death, she became increasingly socially withdrawn and resentful about what she considered the neglect of her earlier quite concerned and attentive friends. Beverly hadn't lived on her own before. She lived with her parents until her marriage to Henry when she was twenty-two. Henry delighted in being the "strong one" in the marriage and was very protective of Beverly. Their two daughters were grown and had left the home. One was married and the other a senior in college. I gave Beverly the assignment of calling one by one the earlier attentive friends until she found one who was available to go out to lunch with her. The following week she came in and described how she gave up after the first friend she called was busy and could not lunch with her. I then engaged her in a dialogue about the meaning of change for her. We discussed at some length the possible consequences of change. We discussed how her life would be different if she stopped isolating herself. We discussed the positive aspects of such a change and some things she would not like about it. As a result of such discussions she became aware of how invested she was in her image of being a tragic figure. Taking a step to socialize with her friends by having a pleasant lunch meant breaking away from this self-imposed enslavement to misery. It also meant moving away from her helpless dependent bid for others to take care of her, which even the most devoted of her friends had grown weary of. Gradually, she relinquished her manipulative and dependent ways of relating in favor of a much fuller and active participation in life.

Encourage mourners to find ways to expiate their guilt. Many bereaved persons will seek out the clergy to share their guilt and make confessions. This is often a crucial step in the healing process and you should encourage those mourners who would be receptive to see their spiritual adviser. Also, the painful ordeal and suffering of the grieving process itself can serve as a type of atonement that alleviates the guilt. Other ways of alleviating guilt have been described earlier and include finding meaningful ways of carrying on the unfinished work of the deceased.

Death of a Parent in Midlife

Losing a parent in midlife can be exceedingly painful. Although the expectation of losing a parent is greater than in earlier periods of the life cycle, it still can come as quite a shock. Many interventions already described will be useful in helping an adult in midlife to grieve for a parent. Surely, it would be important to explore the meaning of the loss for each person at this stage of life. It dramatically brings into focus the fact that one is next in line to die and heightens the awareness of one's own personal death, which is a core feature of the midlife crisis. The unfinished business with that parent, if any, will significantly affect the grieving process. If the death is expected, there may be opportunities to work on these unresolved old conflicts. If death is sudden, the opportunity is lost and the mourner will need help in finding closure some other way. In such circumstances, I have sometimes found that closure can be obtained by such rituals as writing a letter to the deceased parent, or by talking to an empty chair and thereby pretending to have that final good-bye conversation, or sometimes by going to the grave and having a pretend conversation there with the deceased parent.

The unfinished business sometimes may relate to the frustrations of caring for a chronically ill parent. The bereaved may feel terribly guilty about a moment of anger when one was tired or the parent was making impossible demands. Or the terminally ill parent may have lost his/her temper and said some very hurtful things in the midst of his/her pain and suffering. The strategies of facilitating expiation of guilt previously mentioned will be useful in this context.

Death of a Sibling in Midlife

When a sibling dies during midlife the anxiety about one's own mortality may be especially acute because the loss is of a flesh-and-blood member of one's own generation. For an identical twin, the impact can be expected to be especially intense. The death of a sibling can also stir and heighten long-standing rivalries or lead to healing of rifts that have developed during the life cycle. The relationships between siblings may be especially tested and put under a strain when there is an estate to be divided after a parent dies. Some of the wounds and injuries from this process are sometimes carried right to the grave. I have known of instances where siblings have refused to attend the funeral because of a cutoff in the relationship sometimes of many years' duration, so that not even in death does the hatchet get buried. I have also known of siblings who managed to stay close during their adult years and the sense of loss experienced at the death of their brother or sister was profound.

As with other bereavements, before you can assist you will need to understand the significance of the loss to the person and the relationship with the sibling. Ordinarily, grief counselors are likely to be called upon to help in those cases complicated by extreme ambivalence, conflict, and guilt. All the techniques described earlier in this chapter pertaining to acknowledging and resolving the ambivalence will be relevant here.

Summary

During the middle years of adult life the family constellation is subject to radical and unsettling shifts. Children are growing up and leaving home and parents are growing old and dying. Some adults also experience this period as one of profound questioning of deeply held values and beliefs culminating in a midlife crisis. In the context of these developmental stresses this chapter has examined the impact of special losses including the death of children, spouse, parents, and siblings. Guidelines for intervening and helping midlife adults to grieve have been delineated. In the last chapter we will explore ways of assisting the elderly to face losses including their own death at the conclusion of the life cycle.

7

Helping the Elderly to Grieve

I once knew Robert, an elderly man, who never recovered from the death of his beloved wife. He explains in his own words:

> I never thought for a moment that I would outlive Sharon and I don't think she did either. Even after the doctor diagnosed her cancer, I still thought I would go first. She always was looking after me, especially after my eyesight got so bad. She was a trouper. Nothing could keep her down. I guess I didn't want to see just how sick she was because I just always expected her to be here. We were married fifty-two years and since I retired we were always together. We loved to travel and kept on right up to the last year when we just couldn't do it anymore. Every night I talk to her. I guess my friends would think I was crazy if they knew so I don't tell anyone, not even my children. I tell her that I will be with her soon.
>
> —Robert, age seventy-four

Robert died peacefully in his sleep just eleven months after the death of his wife, Sharon, who had been his high-school sweetheart and loving companion for fifty-two years. It could be reasonably said that Robert died of a broken heart. It appears that in response to such painful bereavements and a succession of important losses some elderly people just give up and lose their will to live.

Writers on the aged tend to distinguish between the young-old, those between sixty and seventy-five, and the old-old, those elderly who are seventy-five and over. During this concluding phase of the life cycle some important psychological issues need to be addressed. Erik Erikson referred to the developmental crisis of this final stage as ego integrity vs. despair and disgust.[1] Ego integrity is manifested in "the acceptance of one's own and only life cycle and of the people who have become significant to it as something that had to be and that, by necessity, permitted of no substitutions. It thus means a new different love of one's parents, free of the wish that they should have been different, and an acceptance of the fact that one's life is one's responsibility."[2]

By contrast, despair is revealed in the lack of acceptance of the one and only life cycle accompanied by the feeling that time is short and there is not time to start another life or seek alternative paths. It is very sad when people enter the last phase of their life regretting the life they have lived and feeling there is insufficient time to alter course.

Research and clinical experience point to the tremendous importance of meaningful attachments in the lives of the elderly. Some studies have indicated that having a confiding relationship with at least one person is more important than any other factor in predicting those elderly persons who could remain in the community and those who would be institutionalized. Even the addition of a pet to an elderly person living alone can contribute to a sense of well-being and the feeling of being needed. Developing and maintaining attachments are not always easy for the elderly. A long-debated theory of aging suggests that the natural pattern for the elderly is to disengage socially. According to this theory, there tends to be a gradual withdrawal of contacts with the larger social world and a dropping out of organizations and groups as a result of waning social interest among the elderly. Consequently, the elderly become increasingly socially isolated and lonely. Whether this is the natural pattern or not, there are large numbers of elderly people living isolated and lonely existences. This may partly be due to the geographical separation of many families today. Their lives may be further hampered by problems of ill health, financial strains, and worries. As one seventy-six-year-old man put it, *Old age is not for cowards.*

The elderly who manage to keep active in meaningful pursuits, either work or other fulfilling activities, during their retirement years tend to be healthier and happier. The activity cannot simply be "busy work." It has to be rewarding and enhancing to their self-esteem. The contrast is vividly revealed by the statements of the two elderly men below:

I wish there were more hours in the day. Between the research I am doing on my family history at the library, my music and my hiking, and the other things I try to pack into a day, I feel I am busier than when I was working. I wouldn't trade places with anyone.

—John, age sixty-seven

Nothing has worked out quite the way I expected when I left the company eight years ago. I had so many plans but I never quite got around to doing much of anything. We were going to travel but neither my wife nor I have much interest. I was going to write, something I always wanted to do but I don't even have one page to show for it. Now neither of us is in very good health so there is not much to look forward to. Some days it hardly seems worth it. Where has all the time gone?

—Ronald, age seventy-three

The elderly are exposed to ever-increasing losses. They may have already grieved the deaths of their parents, some of their peers, and perhaps siblings and children as well. With each of these subsequent losses they cannot help but feel that their time is coming closer. Interviews with the elderly reveal that they frequently do mental calculations of their life expectancy based on the longevity of their parents and siblings and if they have lived beyond the expected years they may feel they are living on borrowed time. Elderly couples often will discuss who is likely to survive the other and they may mentally prepare themselves accordingly. In contrast to the younger bereaved, the very elderly bereaved often do not feel motivated to undertake the painful process of mourning since they do not foresee much in the way of future time or opportunities so they do not wish to withdraw the emotional investment in the lost relationship.[3]

Be sensitive to the wishes and genuine needs of the elderly bereaved. We examined earlier in this book how difficult it is for young children to tolerate the painful emotions of mourning and how they need to do grief work in stages as their ego develops. At this final stage of the life cycle, the capacity to mourn has long been developed and many painful losses have already been grieved. Robert perceived his remaining time as short and had never expected to survive his wife. He was in ill health and saw death as a friend; an opportunity to rejoin his wife. He had little incentive or desire to mourn the loss of his wife, as he wished to keep her near to him.

The "image" of the dead spouse plays a vital role in the life of the elderly widow(er)s. Like Robert they may have daily conversations, often secret, with their deceased partner or they may frequently have visual images of the lost person. They may hear their name being called by the deceased spouse and they may consult their partner for guidance. Raphael states, "The widow(er) holds on for the few years left, living on together with the lost person, maybe cherishing this image while awaiting reunion in some form of afterlife."[4] This is not to imply that they do not grieve at all. There may be tremendous pain in the loss and separation; however, the work of reviewing positive and negative memories and the accompanying feelings so that the emotional investment in the lost relationship can be withdrawn is not done. They do not want to let go and move on but rather they seek to keep alive the attachment to the lost spouse. This is certainly not the case with all elderly bereaved, but it is not uncommon especially among those over seventy-five and/or in poor health, where visions of the future are quite limited.

Encourage meaningful social involvement. The differences between the life-styles of elderly men and women are striking. Two-thirds of elderly men live with their spouses, while only one-third of the women have husbands. Only one-sixth of the men live alone or with nonrelatives while one-third of older women live alone or with a nonrelative. After the age of seventy-five, there are 191 females to 100 males.[5] These data point to the likelihood that elderly women will spend a significant portion of their last years alone. This has implications for bereavement counseling. To the extent feasible, given physical and health limitations, the elderly bereaved should be encouraged to interact with their significant others and social environment.

The social involvement will need to be in keeping with their true interests and needs and not just activity for its own sake if it is to have an enhancing effect on self-esteem. In other words just keeping the elderly widow(er) occupied is an inadequate approach. The often degrading "arts and crafts" approach to elderly day care is a prime example. The elderly need meaningful opportunities for interaction with others and not just other elderly but with children and grandchildren. To retire does not equate with retire from life! This need for meaning and purpose is vividly expressed by Joel:

> Ever since Liz died, I find myself mostly just hanging around the house doing things that seem like monstrous chores even though they don't amount to much. Things like emptying the dishwasher, I will avoid for half the day. Occasionally, I go out for a walk with the dog but other than that and grocery shopping I seldom go out. What a bore my everyday existence has become.
>
> —Joel, age seventy-six

Joel, whose life had become increasingly restricted and lonely since his wife died, had been a research scientist prior to his retirement. He rejected most suggestions about ways to increase his social contacts and find more interest and stimulation in his daily life, but he was receptive to the idea of playing chess with some old friends with whom he had lost contact in the recent past. Joel had difficulty motivating himself to follow through, so in counseling sessions it proved helpful to set weekly goals outlining steps he would take between sessions to make these social contacts. He also began to establish daily goals regarding his chores and household responsibilities and experienced a sense of accomplishment as he completed the priorities he set each day. In time he was able to renew his friendships with several men who shared his interest in chess.

Be prepared to encounter hostility among reluctant elderly mourners. Since the elderly often wish to avoid the painful mourning process leading to relinquishing their deceased spouse, they may relate with hostility to helpers. It is not easy to respond therapeutically when you are the object of such hostility. It will be imperative for you to remember that the elderly are relating in a manner quite reasonable and logical given their place in the life cycle. The worst mistake, of course, would be for you to respond in a very personal way to the anger instead of appreciating the context and life situation of the elderly bereaved.

Be prepared for the intense dependency needs expressed by some elderly bereaved. It is common for family members, friends, and even helpers to sometimes be frightened by the intensity of the fear and dependency needs manifested by an elderly widow(er) suddenly alone in the world. You must be clear about the kind of role you can play in the lives of those you seek to help and the limitations of the relationship. This is a firm but compassionate approach since it would be very cruel to mislead the elderly bereaved or to foster false expectations. Since the needs of the elderly are many and call for many different forms of help, it is once again vital to function as a member of a team and to be knowledgeable about the other resources in the community so appropriate referrals can be made. Some may need legal assistance, medical care, social services, or would profit from meeting with a member of the clergy or by participation in a bereavement group. Whatever the need, the helper should establish linkages with those in the community who are a part of the helping network.

Avoid collusion in chronic grief with the excessively dependent. This caution was discussed in the last chapter and bears mention again in relation to helping the elderly bereaved. Both research and clinical experience point to the fact that those who are stuck in a pattern of chronic and excessive dependency are not helped by encouragement of their grieving (typically they have grieved intensely already) and may, in fact, be harmed because it can lead to chronic grief. Instead, it is important to assist them in establishing daily goals to help them in moving forward with their lives. Small accomplishments may provide the needed encouragement to tackle larger challenges.

Some of the chronically dependent who manifest learned helplessness are surprised to find out that they are really quite competent. Others will have known it all along but actually consider their competencies to be more of a curse than a blessing because they have used their pseudohelplessness in a manipulative way to commandeer the resources of others. In the latter case pointing out their capabilities will not be appreciated. This is an important diagnostic clue. It is an indication of angry unwillingness as discussed in chapter 1. The elderly bereaved who respond in such a fashion have been engaged in a lifelong struggle against the exercise of their full capacities. Consequently, they will competitively attempt to defeat the efforts of the helper who in grief counseling encourages the recognition and use of their own solid resources. The elderly bereaved who respond favorably to the helper's delineation of their strengths and capacities may simply have been guided by long-standing false beliefs of their lack of competence. These myths may have been reinforced and perpetuated by significant others. When the central issue is lack of confidence, a goal-setting approach, utilizing small steps and maximizing opportunities for success can be very helpful, along with encouragement and support from helpers and significant others.

Carefully consider the threat of suicide with the elderly be-

reaved. The threat of suicide at any stage of the life cycle should never be taken lightly. The risk factor is especially high, however, with the elderly. It has been found that 25 to 30 percent of all successful suicides in the US involve persons over age sixty-five. If in the course of grief counseling such a threat is made, assessment of suicidal risk should be undertaken by a mental health professional, and the grief counselor or helper should make a referral for a prompt evaluation. In some cases the grief counseling may be done by mental health professionals so a referral may not be necessary. Even then, however, consultation with another mental health professional may be useful in determining suicidal risk and whether the elderly person needs the protective care provided by hospitalization during the period of crisis. These judgments are difficult to make under the best of circumstances since so much is at stake—it is literally a life-and-death decision. This is where you need to remember that you are a member of a team. The bereaved person will be best served if no one person tries heroically to shoulder the whole burden. Many hospitals have psychiatric emergency services that are available around the clock to make such assessments and some even have mobile crisis teams that come to the home to assist in such a situation. It is important for helpers to be cognizant of all such resources in their own communities. The suicidal threat is all the more serious if there are other signs of major depression such as sleep disturbance, poor appetite, weight loss (sometimes it can be manifested by the opposite: compulsive eating, and weight gain), crying spells, low energy, poor concentration, withdrawal, and loss of interest in usual activities. The more of these symptoms present, the more serious is the degree of depression and the associated suicidal risk.

It is crucial to follow up the elderly bereaved. One important study comparing bereavement outcome in younger and older spouses found that the younger spouses (age sixty-three and younger) manifested initially greater intensity of grief than older spouses (age sixty-five and older).[6] After eighteen months, however, the trend was reversed and the older spouses were having the most difficult time. Among the factors cited to account for this finding were the debilitating effects of loneliness and fear for one's personal safety. These findings suggest the importance of regular follow-up over time in counseling the elderly bereaved. The expectation of loss is greater in the elderly, so initially they may not react as strongly to the death as younger spouses but the stress of the bereavement and changes in their life circumstances appear to exact a greater toll over time, which you need to keep in mind in planning interventions. Again, the importance of working collaboratively with other helpers is essential since no one caregiver can meet all of the needs of the elderly bereaved.

Be aware of how grief in old age differs from earlier ages. Caregivers should expect that grief in old age will be of longer duration and that it will often be expressed in somatic symptoms.[7] This may partly reflect the reluctance of the elderly bereaved to undertake the painful mourning process as discussed earlier in this chapter. The painful unexpressed and unresolved grief may then be expressed through somatic symptoms. Declining health in the elderly bereaved can be expected to increase stress greatly and complicate the grief process. Some studies have indicated that negative changes in physical health can be as stressful as the loss of a loved one and sometimes more so if mobility is affected or other drastic restrictions are imposed. When the elderly widow(er) is faced with declining health, you should view the person at risk for poor outcome of bereavement and work as a member of a team in trying to meet the complex needs of the individual.

Identify the elderly bereaved's familiar ways of coping with stress. The old cliché about teaching an old dog new tricks is overstated but in part may apply here. We are capable of learning throughout the life cycle. When we are under stress, however, we tend to lose our ability to be creative and retreat to old familiar ways. Understanding those familiar ways for each particular person in handling stress will enable the helper to encourage and reinforce such adaptive coping strategies.

Be sensitive to the compounding effect of losses. The elderly are living longer than ever before. In some cases, they may outlive one or more of their children. The death of children may be especially hard to accept because the elderly have not prepared themselves for such a loss, as it violates the natural order. The closeness of the attachment, the circumstances of the death, and the degree to which it was expected will all influence the subsequent bereavement. The deaths of siblings and close friends can also be extremely impactful. The loss of long-standing relationships with siblings or friends often intensifies the sense of loneliness and vulnerability to one's own death. The sense of loss may be profound and lead to deep depression. The multiple losses faced by the elderly sometimes have a steeling effect in preparing the elderly in a gradual desensitizing manner for their own death. They can also have a demoralizing effect and lead to a sense of hopelessness and despair. So much depends on preexisting personality patterns, their self-worth, and factors such as their general state of health and financial security. When the losses begin to compound and combine with other stressors in the life of the elderly they may be overwhelming. Although many of the suggestions in this chapter may be useful in providing help to the elderly in these circumstances, you may realistically feel there is little you can do to combat their entrapment in misery. The helpers in these situations may need a great deal of support to avoid becoming demoralized themselves.

In the case of sudden death, the elderly bereaved need frequent opportunities to talk about the death. Although the expectation of loss is greater in the elderly, sudden death can still come as quite a shock. Like the younger bereaved, they need to be provided ample opportunity to go over and over the details of what happened because this allows them to assimilate gradually the sudden and possibly traumatic loss. It is a mistake to say, as the elderly are so often advised in the immediate aftermath of the death, "It does no good to go over and over what happened." In this very early stage it does help the elderly to talk repeatedly about what has happened.

Recognize that family members may benefit from caring for their dying elderly loved one. Clinical experience and research have shown that many families find that having the opportunity to care personally for their dying loved one helps them cope with their subsequent bereavement.[8] It gives them the opportunity to make amends and restitution for any failures or wrongs, real or imagined, in their relationship with the terminally ill family member. If the needs of the critically ill family member are beyond their ability to handle they should be encouraged to seek appropriate medical or hospice care. It is essential that helpers respect the wishes of the family and be sensitive to their needs. While many families might prefer to care for a terminally ill family member at home, in reality they may find such care so demanding and exhausting it actually leads to friction and animosity between the dying patient and family. Such negative interactions with the dying patient complicate subsequent bereavement due to the increased guilt.

It would be a great disservice to such a family to imply that they "should" provide care in the home. The many excellent hospice programs available today offer the family a dignified and compassionate alternative.

Facing One's Own Death

Beginning with the very early conceptions of death in the preschool period, all earlier phases of the life cycle lead naturally to the finality of our existence. Life often assumes a much greater meaning and purpose when we fully appreciate our finitude. Our death is real and will be marked by a specific day on the calendar. All the days leading up to that one assume a special significance. It passes so quickly. A couple of years ago I attended my twenty-fifth year high school reunion. A former schoolmate said, "I just hope the next twenty-five years don't go so fast." I have a feeling they will go even faster. It is hard if not impossible to comprehend fully the end of our existence as we know it. To the extent that we can, it helps us to appreciate life and living all the more.

Elisabeth Kübler-Ross has beautifully and sensitively described the stages of anticipatory mourning that those facing terminal illness work through.[9] During this final stage of life, even among those relatively healthy, the groundwork is laid for facing death by a process of life review.[10] Through review of their many reminiscences, and the accompanying intense emotions, the elderly attempt to make peace with their life as they lived it. Those who succeed achieve what Erikson called ego integrity—"the acceptance of one's one and only life cycle."[11] It is a time of looking back at all earlier phases of the life cycle and although seeing many imperfections, hopefully, one can conclude, "I did as well as I could and I embrace the life that I have lived as mine and mine only." Helpers will have made a significant contribution if they can assist the elderly to review their lives and conclude that they have lived as well as they could. They will not only be more prepared to die but to live more fully the days that remain.

Summary

At the end of the life cycle we are faced with a succession of important losses leading up to our own death. It has often been said that we are not truly prepared to live until we are prepared to die. Although the expectancy of losing those we love increases with age, even in old age losing our cherished companions, children, siblings, and close friends is extremely heartbreaking. This final chapter has reviewed the impact of these special losses and offered suggestions and guidelines for helping the elderly grieve.

Dave (Feb 1996) "The good thing about dying at 39 vs. 70 is that I don't have a lot of regrets. There were things I wanted to do, but, hey, I wasn't given the time to do them." A good way to look at it!

Appendix

A Listing of Some Helping Resources

American Association of Suicidology
2459 S. Ash
Denver, CO 80222
(303) 692-0985

Association of Retired Persons
Widowed Persons Service
1909 K Street, NW
Washington, DC 20049
(202) 872-4700

The Candlelighters Childhood Cancer Foundation
1901 Pennsylvania Avenue, NW
Suite 1001
Washington, DC 20006
(202) 659-5136

The Compassionate Friends (for bereaved parents)
P.O. Box 3696
Oak Brook, IL 60522
(312) 990-0010

The Good Grief Program
Judge Baker Children's Center
295 Longwood Avenue
Boston, MA 02115
(617) 232-8390

MADD (Mothers Against Drunk Drivers)
669 Airport Freeway, Suite 310
Hearst, TX 76053
(817) 268-6233

National Hospice Organization
1901 North Moor Street, Suite 1901
Arlington, VA 22209
(800) 658-8898

National Self-Help Clearing House
33 West 42nd Street
Room 620N
New York, NY 10036
(212) 840-1259

National SIDS Foundation
8240 Professional Place
Landover, MD 20785
(800) 222-SIDS

Parents Without Partners, Inc.
8807 Colesville Road
Silver Spring, MD 20910
(301) 588-9354

Parents of Murdered Children
& Other Survivors of Homicide Victims
100 East 8th Street
Suite B-41
Cincinnati, OH 45202
(513) 721-5683

SHARE (for parents who have experienced the death of a
   very young baby)
SHARE National Office
St. Elizabeth's Hospital
211 South 3rd Street
Belleville, IL 62222
(618) 234-2415

Suicide Prevention Center (for survivors of suicide)
P.O. Box 1393
Dayton, OH 45401-1393
(513) 223-9096

The International THEOS Foundation
(They Help Each Other Spiritually—
   for the widowed)
1301 Clark Building
717 Liberty Avenue
Pittsburgh, PA 15222
(412) 471-7779

Notes

Chapter 1: The Need to Grieve throughout the Life Cycle

1. M. Wolfenstein, "How Is Mourning Possible?" *Psychoanalytic Study of the Child* 21 (1966): 93–123.
2. R. A. Furman, "Death and the Young Child: Some Preliminary Considerations," *Psychoanalytic Study of the Child* 19 (1964): 321–33. See also J. Bowlby, "Grief and Mourning in Infancy and Early Childhood," *Psychoanalytic Study of the Child* 15 (1960): 9–52.
3. J. Worden, *Grief Counseling and Grief Therapy* (New York: Springer Publishing Company, 1982), p. 102.
4. J. Bowlby, *The Making and Breaking of Affectional Bonds* (London: Tavistock Publications, 1979).
5. Worden, *Grief Counseling*, p. 11.
6. S. S. Fox, *Good Grief: Helping Groups of Children When a Friend Dies* (Boston: New England Association for the Education of Young Children, 1985).
7. Worden, *Grief Counseling*, p. 41.
8. Ibid.
9. W. Bonime, *Collaborative Psychoanalysis* (Teaneck: Fairleigh Dickinson University Press, 1989), pp. 200–201.
10. D. W. Krueger, "Psychotherapy of Adult Patients with Problems of Parental Loss in Childhood," *Current Concepts in Psychiatry* 4 (1978): 2–7.
11. E. K. Rynearson, "Psychotherapy of Pathologic Grief," *Psychatric Clinics of North America* 10 (1987): 487–99.
12. Worden, *Grief Counseling*, p. 65.

13. G. W. Brown and T. Harris, *Social Origins of Depression: A Study of Psychiatric Disorder in Women* (London: Tavistock Publications, 1978), pp. 173–79.
14. E. Furman, *A Child's Parent Dies: Studies in Childhood Bereavement* (New Haven: Yale University Press, 1974), p. 21.
15. N. Garmezy and M. Rutter, eds., *Stress, Coping, and Development in Children* (New York: McGraw-Hill Book Company, 1983), p. 2.
16. J. M. Lewis, *To Be a Therapist* (New York: Brunner/Mazel, 1978), p. 31.
17. J. Bowlby and C. M. Parkes, "Separation and Loss within the Family," in E. J. Anthony and C. Koupernik, eds., *The Child in His Family* (New York: John Wiley and Sons, 1970), p. 208.
18. T. A. Rando, *Grief, Dying, and Death: Clinical Interventions for Caregivers* (Champaign: Research Press Company, 1984), p. 114.
19. C. M. Parkes and R. W. Weiss, *Recovery From Bereavement* (New York: Basic Books, 1983), p. 228.

Chapter 2: Helping Preschool Children to Grieve

1. J. Bowlby, *Attachment and Loss: Loss, Sadness, and Depression* (Vol. 3) (New York: Basic Books, 1980), p. 9.
2. E. H. Erikson, *Identity and the Life Cycle* (New York: International Universities Press, 1959), p. 55.
3. E. Becker, *The Denial of Death* (New York: Free Press, 1973), pp. 11–24.
4. S. Fraiberg, *The Magic Years—Understanding and Handling the Problems of Early Childhood* (New York: Charles Scribner's, 1959), 179–202.
5. W. Bonime, personal communication, April 9, 1985.
6. E. A. Grollman, *Explaining Death to Children* (Boston: Beacon Press, 1967), p. 10.
7. Ibid., p. 17.
8. J. C. Mills and R. J. Crowley, *Therapeutic Metaphors for Children and the Child Within* (New York: Brunner/Mazel, 1986).
9. Ibid., p. 76.

10. W. Van Ornum and J. B. Mordock, *Crisis Counseling with Children and Adolescents* (New York: Continuum, 1988), pp. 61–67.
11. E. Furman, *A Child's Parent Dies: Studies in Childhood Bereavement* (New Haven: Yale University Press, 1974), p. 17.
12. L. C. Terr, "Forbidden Games," *Journal of the American Academy of Child Psychiatry* 20 (1981): 741–60.

Chapter 3: Helping School-Age Children to Grieve

1. E. H. Erikson, *Identity and the Life Cycle* (New York: International Universities Press, 1959), p. 82.
2. J. Piaget, *Judgment and Reasoning in the Child* (New York: Harcourt Brace, 1928).
3. S. S. Fox, *Good Grief: Helping Groups of Children When a Friend Dies* (Boston: New England Association for the Education of Young Children, 1985).
4. Wolfenstein, "How Is Mourning Possible?" pp. 93–123.
5. Van Ornum and Mordock, *Crisis Counseling with Children*, p. 63.
6. H. Deutsch, "The Absence of Grief," *The Psychoanalytic Quarterly* 6 (1937): 12–22.
7. H. Nagera, *The Developmental Approach to Childhood Psychopathology* (New York: Jason Aronson, 1981), 363–404.
8. B. Raphael, *The Anatomy of Bereavement* (New York: Basic Books, 1983), p. 99.
9. D. A. Crenshaw, J. Boswell, R. Guare, and C. J. Yingling, "Intensive Psychotherapy of Repeatedly and Severely Traumatized Children," *Residential Group Care and Treatment* 3 (1986): 17–36.
10. L. Peller, "Libidinal Phases, Ego Development, and Play," *Psychoanalytic Study of the Child* 9 (1954): 178–97.
11. V. Volkan, "The Linking Objects of Pathological Mourners," *Archives of General Psychiatry* 27 (1972): 215–21.
12. Deutsch, "Absence of Grief," pp. 12–22.
13. Raphael, *Bereavement*, p. 108.
14. R. Baker, *Growing Up* (New York: Signet, 1984), p. 81.

Chapter 4: Helping Adolescents to Grieve

1. J. Blume, *Tiger Eyes* (Scarsdale: Bradbury Press, 1981), p. 3.
2. A. K. Gordon, "The Tattered Cloak of Immortality," in C. A. Corr and J. N. McNeil, eds., *Adolescence and Death* (New York: Springer Publishing Company, 1986), p. 22.
3. T. A. Rando, *Grief, Dying, and Death: Clinical Interventions for Caregivers* (Champaign: Research Press Company, 1984), p. 87.
4. C. Gapes, "A Study of Bereaved Adolescents and Their Church Group," manuscript, 1982.
5. Raphael, *Bereavement*, pp. 162–63. See also S. J. Fleming and R. Adolph, "Helping Bereaved Adolescents: Needs and Responses," in C. A. Corr and J. N. McNeil, eds., *Adolescence and Death* (New York: Springer Publishing Company, 1986), pp. 97–118.
6. M. A. Sklansky, "The Pubescent Years: Eleven to Fourteen," in S. I. Greenspan and G. H. Pollock, eds., *The Course of Life, Vol. 2: Latency, Adolescence, and Youth* (Washington, DC: US Department of Health and Human Services, 1980), pp. 265–92.
7. A. Freud, "Adolescence," *Psychoanalytic Study of the Child* 13 (1958): 279–95.
8. H. Kohut, *The Analysis of the Self* (New York: International Universities Press, 1971).
9. D. Offer and J. B. Offer, *From Teenage to Young Manhood* (New York: Basic Books, 1975).
10. P. Blos, "The Second Individuation Process of Adolescence," *Psychoanalytic Study of the Child* 22 (1967): 162–68.
11. M. Mahler, "Thoughts about Development and Individuation," *Psychoanalytic Study of the Child* 8 (1963): 307–27.
12. Sklansky, "Pubescent Years," in S. I. Greenspan and G. H. Pollock, eds, *The Course of Life, Vol. 2*, p. 280.
13. H. R. Beiser, "Ages Eleven to Fourteen," in Greenspan and Pollock, eds., *The Course of Life, Vol. 2*, p. 299.
14. Beiser, "Ages Eleven to Fourteen." In Greenspan and Pollock, eds., *The Course of Life, Vol. 2*, p. 299.
15. J. D. Nospitz, "Disturbances in Early Adolescent Develop-

ment," in Greenspan and Pollock, eds., *The Course of Life, Vol. 2*, pp. 309–56.

16. Nospitz, "Disturbances in Early Adolescent Development," in Greenspan and Pollock, eds., *The Course of Life, Vol. 2*, p. 318.

17. Rando, *Grief, Dying, and Death*, p. 86.

18. Raphael, *Bereavement*, p. 152.

19. W. Bonime, *Collaborative Psychoanalysis* (Teaneck: Fairleigh Dickinson University Press, 1989), p. 159.

20. W. F. Connell, R. E. Stroobant, E. E. Sinclair, R. W. Connell, and K. W. Rogers, *Twelve to Twenty: Studies of City Youth* (Sidney: Hicks, Smith & Sons, 1975).

21. Fleming and Adolph, "Helping Bereaved Adolescents," pp. 97–118.

22. C. Cain (director), *The Stone Boy* (film) (Los Angeles: Twentieth Century-Fox Entertainment, 1984).

23. D. E. Balk, "Sibling Death During Adolescence: Self-concept and Bereavement Reactions," doctoral dissertation, University of Illinois, Champaign-Urbana, 1981.

24. Bonime, *Collaborative Psychoanalysis*, p. 43.

25. Raphael, *Bereavement*, p. 146.

26. S. P. Bank and M. D. Kahn, *The Sibling Bond* (New York: Basic Books, 1982), p. 19.

27. Sklansky, "Pubescent Years," pp. 281–82.

Chapter 5: Helping Young Adults to Grieve

1. E. H. Erikson, *Identity and the Life Cycle* (New York: International Universities Press, 1959), p. 95.

2. R. L. Gould, "Transformational Tasks in Adulthood," in S. I. Greenspan and G. H. Pollock, eds., *The Course of Life, Vol. 3: Adulthood and the Aging Process* (Washington, DC: US Department of Health and Human Services, 1981), pp. 55–90.

3. S. J. Fleming and R. Adolph, "Helping Bereaved Adolescents: Needs and Responses," in C. A. Corr and J. N. McNeil, eds., *Adolescence and Death* (New York: Springer Publishing Company, 1986), pp. 97–118.

4. D. C. Maddison and W. L. Walker, "Factors Affecting the Outcome of Conjugal Bereavement," *British Journal of Psychiatry* 113 (1967): 1057–67. See also D. C. Maddison, A. Viola, and W. L. Walker, "Further Studies in Conjugal Bereavement," *Australian and New Zealand Journal of Psychiatry* 3 (1969): 63–66.

5. Bowlby and Parkes, "Separation and Loss within the Family," p. 208.

6. B. Raphael, "Preventive Intervention with the Recently Bereaved," *Archives of General Psychiatry* 34 (1977): 1450–54. See also B. Raphael, "Mourning and the Prevention of Melancholia," *British Journal of Medical Psychiatry* 51 (1978): 303–10.

7. J. Worden, *Grief Counseling and Grief Therapy* (New York: Springer Publishing Company, 1982), p. 46.

8. Raphael, *Bereavement,* p. 274.

9. A. C. Cain and B. S. Cain, "On Replacing a Child," *Journal of the American Academy of Child Psychiatry* 3 (1964): 433–56.

10. L. G. Peppers and R. J. Knapp, *Motherhood and Mourning* (New York: Praeger, 1980).

11. Raphael, *Bereavement,* p. 236.

12. Cain and Cain, "Replacing a Child," pp. 433–56.

13. Raphael, *Bereavement,* p. 238.

14. Ibid., p. 242.

15. T. A. Rando, *Parental Loss of a Child* (Champaign: Research Press Company), 1986, pp. 254–55.

16. Raphael, *Bereavement,* pp. 242–47.

17. J. B. Beckwith, *The Sudden Infant Death Syndrome,* revised edition (Washington, DC: DHEW Publication No. HSA 75–5137, US Government Printing Office, 1978).

18. J. Taylor, J. DeFrain, and L. Ernst, "Sudden Infant Syndrome," in T. A. Rando, ed., *Parental Loss of a Child* (Champaign: Research Press Company, 1986), p. 165.

Chapter 6: Helping Adults in Midlife to Grieve

1. R. L. Gould, "Transformational Tasks in Adulthood," in Greenspan and Pollock, eds., *The Course of Life, Vol. 3,* pp. 55–90.

2. E. H. Erikson, *Identity and the Life Cycle* (New York: International Universities Press, 1959), p. 97.
3. Gould, *Transformational Tasks,* p. 77.
4. E. Jaques, "The Midlife Crisis," in Greenspan and Pollock, eds., *The Course of Life, Vol. 3,* pp. 1–24.
5. C. M. Parkes and R. S. Weiss, *Recovery from Bereavement* (New York: Basic Books, 1983), p. 239.
6. R. Redford (director), *Ordinary People* (film) (Hollywood: Paramount Pictures, 1980).
7. R. Reiner (director), *Stand by Me* (film) (Burbank: Columbia Pictures, 1986).
8. Gould, *Transformational Tasks,* pp. 77–78.
9. Parkes and Weiss, *Recovery from Bereavement,* pp. 237–46.
10. Ibid., pp. 233–35.
11. Bonime, *Collaborative Psychoanalysis,* p. 155.
12. Parkes and Weiss, *Recovery from Bereavement,* p. 246.

Chapter 7: Helping the Elderly to Grieve

1. E. H. Erikson, *Identity and the Life Cycle* (New York: International Universities Press, 1959), p. 97.
2. Ibid., p. 98.
3. Raphael, *Bereavement,* p. 314.
4. Ibid., pp. 313–14.
5. E. W. Busse, "Old Age," in Greenspan and Pollock, eds., *The Course of Life, Vol. 3,* pp. 519–44.
6. C. M. Sanders, "Comparison of Younger and Older Spouses in Bereavement Outcome," *Omega: Journal of Death and Dying* 11 (1980–81): 217–32.
7. B. E. Skelskie, "An Exploratory Study of Grief in Old Age," *Smith College Studies in Social Work* 45 (1975): 159–82.
8. Parkes and Weiss, *Recovery from Bereavement,* p. 234.
9. E. Kübler-Ross, *On Death and Dying* (New York: Macmillan, 1968), pp. 38–137.
10. R. Butler, "The Life Review: An Interpretation of Reminiscence in the Aged," *Psychiatry* 3 (1963): 65–76.
11. Erikson, *Identity,* p. 191.